Burnet Landreth

Market Gardening and Farm Notes

Experiences and observations in the garden and field, of interest to the amateur gardener, trucker and farmer

Burnet Landreth

Market Gardening and Farm Notes

Experiences and observations in the garden and field, of interest to the amateur gardener, trucker and farmer

ISBN/EAN: 9783337068868

Printed in Europe, USA, Canada, Australia, Japan

Cover: Foto ©Lupo / pixelio.de

More available books at **www.hansebooks.com**

MARKET GARDENING

AND

FARM NOTES

Experiences and Observations

IN THE GARDEN AND FIELD, OF INTEREST TO THE

AMATEUR GARDENER, TRUCKER AND FARMER

BY

BURNET LANDRETH

Chief Bureau of Agriculture Centennial Inter-National Exhibition,
Officier du Merite Agricole de France.

NEW YORK
ORANGE JUDD COMPANY
1893

COPYRIGHT, 1892,
BY ORANGE JUDD COMPANY

CONTENTS.

CHAPTER I.
	Page.
Market Gardening	1

CHAPTER II.
| Location and Soils | 17 |

CHAPTER III.
| The Science of Gardening | 22 |

CHAPTER IV.
| Chemistry of the Garden | 30 |

CHAPTER V.
| Stable Manure, Compost and Commercial Fertilizers | 35 |

CHAPTER VI.
| Sowing Seeds | 41 |

CHAPTER VII.
| Germination | 44 |

CHAPTER VIII.
| Transplanting | 61 |

CHAPTER IX.
| Succession, or the Rotation of Crops | 64 |

CHAPTER X.
| Garden Insects | 57 |

CHAPTER XI.
| Diseases of Garden Vegetable | 65 |

MARKET GARDENING.

CHAPTER XII.
Heredity in Plants.................................... 69

CHAPTER XIII.
Saving Seed.. 73

CHAPTER XIV.
Seedsmen's Novelties and Responsibilities............. 78

CHAPTER XV.
Weeds.. 82

CHAPTER XVI.
Hotbeds and Cold Frames.............................. 84

CHAPTER XVII.
Market Gardening Under Glass......................... 94

CHAPTER XVIII.
Celery... 113

CHAPTER XIX.
Onion Culture.. 125

CHAPTER XX.
Mushroom Culture..................................... 135

CHAPTER XXI.
Roots for Stock Feeding.............................. 140

CHAPTER XXII.
Packing and Shipping Vegetables...................... 164

CHAPTER XXIII.
Implements for the Farm and Garden................... 169

CHAPTER XXIV.
A Half-Acre Garden................................... 182

CHAPTER XXV.
Calendar Indicating Operations for the Northern and Southern States................................... 185

CHAPTER XXVI.
The Grass Question................................... 198

Index.. 214

MARKET GARDENING.

CHAPTER I.

Market Gardening.

Though this volume is written for the amateur, or family gardener, indeed, to be more precise, for the novice in gardening, it may, however, fall into the hands of more experienced persons, inclined to make a venture in *gardening for profit,* and, accordingly, it may not be out of place to make some remarks upon subjects connected with growing vegetables for sale. The last United States Census Bureau has issued a bulletin on Truck Farming, from which the writer makes the following extracts. Upward of $100,000,000 is invested in this industry, the annual products reaching a value of $75,000,000, the product of 534,440 acres of land.

The annual expenditures for fertilizers being.................$10,000,000
The cost of seeds used amounting to............................ $1,420,633
The number of men employed being.............................. 216,765
The number of women employed being........................... 9,254
The number of children employed being 14,874
The number of horses and mules employed being............. 75,800
The value of the implements used being $8,971,000

For convenience of tabulation the States are divided into districts. The following is a summary of the number of acres under cultivation for truck farming purposes, and the value of products raised, given by districts, is as follows:

Districts.	Acres.	Value of products.
New England	6,838	$3,184,218
Philadelphia	108,135	21,102,521
Peninsular	25,714	2,413,648
Norfolk	45,375	4,692,859
Baltimore	37,181	3,784,696
South Atlantic	111,441	13,183,516
Mississippi Valley	36,180	4,982,579
Southwest	36,889	4,979,783
Central	107,414	15,432,223
Northwest	1,083	204,791
Mountain	3,833	531,976
Pacific Coast	14,357	2,024,345
	534,440	$76,517,155

In the Philadelphia district, which includes Pennsylvania, New Jersey and New York, there are employed 69,000 men at an average cost for daily wages of $1.19; the annual production being of the value of $21,000,000.

The next district of importance, extending over the State of Ohio as far as Wisconsin, is known as the Central, wherein are employed 34,000 men, at an average wages cost of $1.16 per day, and producing an annual valuation of $15,500,000.

The South Atlantic district is the third in importance, having an output of $13,000,000 and employing 31,000 men, women and children at an average daily wages of eighty-five cents.

As an example of the market gardening output at Norfolk, Va., it may be interesting to note the extent of some of the shipments made from that city in one year.

Cabbage	347,000	barrels.
Kale	178,000	"
Onions	4,800	"
Radishes	4,200	"
Irish potatoes	325,000	"
Sweet potatoes	255,000	"
Spinach	123,000	"
Beans	80,000	boxes.
Cucumbers	46,000	"
Tomatoes	350,000	"

In addition to the above there were shipped from the same city almost 1,000,000 watermelons. And yet it was considered a poor year.

From the city of Mobile, in the next year, the shipments were:

Crates of cabbage	58,309
Boxes of beans	46,178
Boxes of peas	1,278
Boxes of tomatoes	2,695
Barrels of potatoes	78,924
Other market garden products	$458,000

The Philadelphia district, the Central district, and the South Atlantic district are only three of twelve districts as laid out by the Census Bureau, that of California giving an annual production of over $4,000,000, and yet there is room for the productions of all, amounting to $76,000,000, and no doubt in a few years that sum will be doubled, for everything soon doubles in this land of phenomenal progress.

The unprecedented development in the Carolinas and Gulf States of the business of growing vegetables for autumn and winter shipment to the cities of the North, to be from those active centers more widely distributed among the densely populated districts of the Middle, Western and New England States, has been one of the surprises in modern agriculture.

Formerly esculent vegetables could be divided into classes, and a period named covering the time of sale of each class—as, for example, peas were only offered during May, June and July, and so with cucumbers, tomatoes, egg plants and beans, they all had their seasons, and, when they were past, only those people who had greenhouses could expect more until the return of the corresponding season the following year, but now that is a condition of the past, for Georgia and Florida, with their evergreen productiveness, have been able to revolutionize the old conditions, by sending to the northern cities, even when snow clad and ice bound, the fruits of balmy summer.

From such a perennial field there are now offered, at all times, vegetables which at first surprised the observers and were only used by epicures, but which now have become a necessity, not only on the table of the rich and well-to-do, but of every hotel and restaurant.

Thus, thanks especially to Florida, the general public of the whole country have luxuries at their command which their ancestors never even hoped to obtain, and the now familiar products of Florida have brought that State more prominently to the notice of the Northern people than has the wheat and corn of any Western State made its name known, for grain products do not carry with them their own identifications as do cucumbers in March, egg plants in December and January, tomatoes from January to March, cauliflower in March and April.

The value of the output of winter vegetables from Georgia and Florida, and the value of the quantity consumed by the winter guests of the hotels, tips the scale at a valuation of several millions of dollars, a large sum considering that the cultivation is yet in its infancy, for the production of vegetables, in Florida especially, is certain to develop to an immense degree, as no competition can come from a more southern district. The profits of the Norfolk truckers were cut by the Charleston and Savannah market gardeners, and they, in turn, by the Florida cultivators, but the Gulf is south of Florida, so competition stops, or becomes merely interstate, there being no neighbors southwardly to compete with earlier productions.

Market gardening may be termed commercial gardening, as the operator must, to a certain extent, be a merchant, fully alive to the import of fluctuating prices, and quick to change his point of shipment or his consignee.

The market gardener, filling a multiform position as a cultivator of the soil to an intense degree, as a careful packer of products in such a manner as to make his goods attractive and saleable, as a shipper and a close reader of market intelligence, must have the best agricultural appliances and commercial aids, none of which can be procured without money, consequently the subject of capital is one of considerable importance.

Capital.—The capital of a market gardener should be estimated by his available cash, compared with the number of his acres, and, as, in other things, opinions vary, so do the estimates of practical gardeners, some being satisfied to live on inexpensive land far removed from market, and use what others would term an incomplete line of implements, and be satisfied with what nature develops in the ordinary routine of their business, while others, more progressive, locate in the outskirts of great cities, consequently upon high-priced land, and have everything new in the way of labor-saving appliances.

The first class of gardeners may be termed experimental farmers, men tired of the humdrum rotation of farm processes and small profits, men looking for a paying diversification of their agricultural interests. Their expenses for appliances are not great, as they have already on hand the usual stock of farm tools, requiring only one or two seed drills, a small addition to their cultivating implements, and a few tons of fertilizers. Their laborers and teams are always on hand for the working of moderate areas. In addition to their usual expenses of the farm, they would not need to have a cash capital of beyond twenty to twenty-five dollars per acre for the area in truck. Other men, in ordinary farming districts, purchasing or renting land, especially for market gardening, taking only improved land of suitable aspect, soil and situation, and counting in cost of building, appliances and labor, would require a cash capital of eighty to one hundred dollars per acre. For example, a beginner in market gardening in South Jersey, on a five-acre patch, would need five hundred dollars to set up the business and run it until his shipments began to return him money. With the purpose of securing information on this interesting point, the writer asked for estimates from market gardeners in different localities, and the result has been that from Florida the reports of the necessary capital per acre in land or its rental (not of labor), fertilizers, tools, implements, seed and all the appliances, average ninety-five dollars, from Texas forty-five, from Illinois seventy dollars; from the Norfolk district of Virginia the reports vary from seventy-five to one hundred and twenty-five dollars, according to location, and from Long Island, New York, the average of estimates at the east end are seventy-five, and, at the west end, one hundred and fifty dollars.

Market gardeners, living ten miles out of Philadelphia, on tracts of twenty and thirty acres, devoting all their land and energies to growing vegetables, sometimes paying forty dollars per acre for rent, estimate that the necessary capital averages from two hundred to three hundred dollars per acre, according to the amount of truck grown in hotbeds. These same men calculate the profits to be from one hundred and fifty dollars to two hundred and fifty dollars per acre.

Very different is the case on the immediate outskirts of Philadelphia, and other large cities, with the five and ten acre gardeners, employing several men to the acre, sometimes a larger force, where high rents, high wages, intense manuring and expensive forcing-houses combine to swell the expenses to an astonishing degree, often over six or seven hundred dollars per acre being absorbed the first year, and without which ready capital at command the suburban cultivator would be driven to the wall before the close of the first season, as he works under heavy expenses, and he must have ready cash to meet them, especially if the first season be an unprofitable one. Of course, the six or seven hundred dollars per acre which may be expended the first year by a gardener having forcing houses, with all the entailed expenses, need not be repeated the second, not more than one-half of it, and, indeed, it is absolutely necessary to reduce expenses, as the profit in trucking would not warrant such an annual cash outlay; but what would be thought of an annual *rental* of six hundred dollars per acre, which is the rate charged for a market garden which the writer visited in the outskirts of Paris, France.

Location.—Alluvial soils with gravel subsoil are best for garden vegetables, but one finds many exceptions, as nearly pure clays, on the one hand, and white, apparently inert, sands, on the other, have been made to yield a satisfactory return for labor and time put upon them. Of course, a light soil means early crops, and a clay soil later ones. It may be said that in the South early crops always pay the best, but in the North late crops are often the most profitable, as they come in after the market has ceased to be glutted. Location is of the utmost importance, as, evidently, it would be idle to expect success where the means of regular and prompt shipment to market are not within reach, hence location may be looked upon as an indispensable preliminary. But it is not all, for the nature of the soil is an even more important one, as without a soil, productive naturally, or with artificial stimulation, it matters little what the transportation facilities may be.

Transportation.—From many communications which the writer has received, he gathers that the inquirers imagine, because they are on a railroad a few hours or a hundred miles or so from a shipping point, that they are well placed for market gardening. This is a grave mistake. True the railroad car or the steamer which is to receive articles so perishable as fruit and garden vegetables for transportation, should be near at hand, as hauling over rough country roads should be avoided as much as possible, and transshipment from cars to boat, or vice-versa, is to be dreaded, as every disturbance is promotive of decay, and attended by expense in some shape or other, as well as liable to cause delay. The writer would impress upon all not to embark in the business of market gardening and small fruit growing, however much they may be tempted by ready transportation, unless they are, themselves, favorably located for such pursuits; for a good location means not only transportation, but condition of soil, and availability of labor.

There are other crops besides garden vegetables and fruit which will, in many locations, pay more certainly, and, as a necessary result, more fully, in the end—just as the moderate man, who is content with six per cent. well secured on land, fares better, finally, than he who grasps at two and one-half per cent. a month on doubtful paper.

Where transportation, climate, soil, ability to command labor and manure, unite to point out any special spot as well adapted to the object, the next point of inquiry is, which crops are the best to grow? This is, also, an all-important subject to be considered, inasmuch as the facility for shipment may be all that is desirable, but the distance from market too great to afford hope for the successful transportation of the more perishable class of products. Within fifty to sixty hours of market by rail or boat, delicate fruits and comparatively perishable culinary vegetables may be moved successfully, but beyond that distance danger of decay increases, and the business assumes too much the complexion of a lottery, where the blanks far out-number the prizes. A shipment, eighty hours on its travels, may occasionally reach its destination and pay largely, but the loss on other shipments which may arrive at destination heated and decayed will more than absorb previous profits.

Much, however, depends on the season, as, for example, a shipment from Florida to the North during the winter months will, if not frozen in transit, carry twice as long as in spring or autumn, and three times as long as in summer. Hence it will be seen that not only must there exist certain conditions as respects facility for shipment, but the adoption of the locality, with reference to distance from market, must be carefully considered, before deciding as to the crops to be grown.

With such a location as Burlington county, New Jersey, where the writer has a farm, and where have congregated so vast a number of "truckers," as they are popularly called, and small fruit growers, attracted by the light kindly soils, admitting of tillage early in the spring, and the markets of New York and Philadelphia in close proximity, where gathering of perishable vegetables and picking of fruit may be pursued till sunset, and the next morning find them in market, everything which the climate admits may be successfully produced. Still further south, as in the vicinity of Norfolk, Wilmington and Savannah, other cultivators are pursuing market gardening on a larger scale, and, although the transportation is more expensive and of longer duration, these points are still within easy reach of market, while the earlier season in which crops are produced is a compensation for increased expenses. It may not be fully realized by all persons into whose hands this work may fall, that the time or season in which a vegetable delicacy or choice fruit is placed in market has an important influence on the price. In our large commercial and manufacturing cities where wealth has concentrated, and where abound families who live regardless of expenditures, fabulous prices are freely paid for vegetables and fruits to please the palate or adorn the table.

Products.—At Norfolk are grown extra early peas in great quantity, string or snap short beans, early cucumbers, tomatoes, kale, cabbage, spinach, early squash and early potatoes, and other articles of minor importance. Berry culture is also pursued there, and large quantities of strawberries reach the Northern markets from that quarter, and several weeks before those grown near Philadelphia are ripe. Melons also find there a congenial soil along rivers and water-courses, and where ready means of transportation admit of carriage of bulky articles at reasonable rates. To illustrate the extent to which trucking at Norfolk is pursued may be cited the spinach crop grown there, which annually takes one hundred thousand pounds of seed to sow the land.

Still further south, from the ports of Charleston and Savannah, come to us in advance of those of Norfolk, peas, beans, asparagus, cucumbers, cabbage, potatoes and berries.

But is it necessary to profitable gardening that there should be great variety? On this subject there are two distinct views, one set of men directing their energies to the production of a limited variety, aiming to grow and ship those well. Such a system affords a longer time for planting and culture, the mind not being harassed by the conflicting claims of many crops, the few which grow being harvested, affording an opportunity to plan for the future and rest from the labors of the past. A second set of cultivators planting more or less of everything, at every season, always planting, seeding, marketing, a never-ceasing round of labor and anxiety. This system, however, seems to be one which, by its very diversification, offers the best hope of profit, as the cultivator does not carry all his eggs in one basket, nor in several, but in many.

With the seven millions of people of Philadelphia, New York, Boston, St. Louis and Chicago, and the many millions more in other cities and towns which look to these great distributing markets for supplies, there is, at seasonable seasons, little fear of gorging the markets of the country if the fruit and vegetables be well chosen and well packed. The reader will observe the cautious use of the expression *seasonable season*, as, of course, no Southern grower of tomatoes, cucumbers, egg plant or other garden products would expect to find a market for his goods in Northern cities when those markets were in receipt of the same class of garden truck from territory adjacent, the products of which would be fresher and cheaper than those from distant points. The shipper of fruits and vegetables from the South, attempting to cope with the garden States of New Jersey and Delaware, when their products are being sent to market, would only have his trouble for his pay

It will be perceived, from the reference to the great distributing markets, that they must be reached by several channels or lines of transportation. In the East along the seaboard by steamer or coast railway lines from points as far south as Key West, inland up to St. Louis, Chicago, Detroit, Minneapolis, St. Paul, Cincinnati, Cleveland, by the various railways of the Mississippi Valley, from gardening sections of Louisiana, Alabama, Mississippi, Tennessee, further west still on north and south lines from Texas and Arkansas. In continuation of the remarks on the limited or comprehensive systems of cropping, it may be added that there are two extremes.

First:—That of too fine a concentration, the reduction of the varieties to a very few, the carrying of all of the eggs in one basket, a glutted market of such fruits and vegetables, sweeping away all hopes of profit, with no resources in other crops. If the cultivator is at a distance, requiring over a day or two to reach the larger markets, then four or five varieties which develop well should be planted. The nearer the cultivator is to market, the greater the range of varieties he can ship successfully.

Second:—That of too great diversification and the undertaking to grow too many kinds of vegetables, requiring widely different conditions of soil and climate, the land, perhaps, being very favorable to some, and to others not adapted at all.

If growers in the Southern States would continue to raise, each year, such varieties as have proved adapted to their soil and location, and avoid overcropping with such sorts, which, by accident, paid the largest return the preceding season, their average yearly return would certainly be better. To illustrate this more clearly, it may be well to note a circumstance which occurred during the spring of 1890. The spring before, Philadelphia received a limited supply of from one hundred to two hundred quarts per day of strawberries from Florida, very early, and very good, and they found ready sale at from sixty cents to one dollar per quart, the consequence being the setting out in Florida of a very largely increased acreage of strawberry plants. Now, what was the result? The receipts from the same section the spring of 1891 ran from one thousand to two thousand quarts per day, and they were retailed through the streets by hawkers at fifteen to eighteen cents per quart, the results of over-production.

Large quantities of new potatoes reach the markets of New York and Philadelphia from Bermuda, Charleston, Savannah, Florida, and, still later, but before Northern crops mature, from Virginia and Maryland, and there is room for more, at paying prices, and they who present them early, of good sorts and in good condition, need not apprehend a want of customers.

Florida, however, seems to be destined to be the market garden of the Atlantic States, as the gardening year there is one of almost continued sowing and harvesting. So unusual are the conditions that they have upset all the usual gardening records of the seasons, for the Florida trucker, working throughout the length of a peninsula of two hundred miles, is sowing nearly every kind of seed in every month, and marketing crops out of their usual seasons. For instance, egg plant is sown in August, onion seed in October, tomato seed in November, and so on. The ordinary routine of sowing has been disturbed, and yet everything appears to grow in profusion and to perfection.

Fertilizers.—The subject of fertilizers is one which looms up boldly and expensively when considering the culture of garden products, especially those designed for early maturity. The writer is asked every day what kind of manure is best for this or that crop. Is guano good? Do you use superphosphate? He can only answer in general terms. Yes, they are all good, if made by reliable parties; but which is most valuable in respect to cost and effects produced will depend, in no small degree, on each particular surrounding. In localities where horses and cattle abound, stable manures will usually be attainable at moderate prices; especially will this be the case where gardening is not pursued to a large extent, and the sale of manure is mainly to ordinary farmers, who are not accustomed to paying high prices.

On the other hand, around Philadelphia, for instance, the charge for the article in question is fearfully exorbitant, the price it generally commands at that city is seventy cents per small cartload, delivered on board boat or car. Eight such loads can readily be drawn by two good horses, as has frequently been done at Bloomsdale. Under such conditions of expense, the gardener must resort to all the fertilizers within reach, hoping to find something less expensive, but all are generally quite costly.

To give an idea of the expenditure for manure when intense effects are to be produced, the writer will add that one year the order for Bloomsdale and Reedland Farms, six hundred and fifty acres, reached the sum of twenty thousand dollars. When stable manure cannot be had, as in a sparsely settled country, wood ashes may play an important part, and, if artificial fertilizers need to be bought, superphosphate and Peruvian guano will come in as useful adjuncts to home manure, compost and green crops, plowed under. Baugh's superphosphate is in good repute in Philadelphia, and we feel warranted to say, from our own experience, that it is reliable. In short, all organic matter, and nearly every substance that decomposes, is able, if rightly applied, to stimulate vegetable growth. But let it be observed, for on this fact much depends, the product, in respect to earliness, is influenced in proportion to the quality and quantity of manure applied. The truck gardeners of Philadelphia understand this well, and place in market, by the aid of excessive application of excrementitious matter, cabbage, lettuce, radish, beets, long before they are fit for use in private gardens, where such rank manures would not be countenanced, and, of course, with extra early products, they reap large profits.

It is a good plan to prepare manure in advance of the season of demand, by making compost heaps, as they are called, which can be drawn upon as needed, without having to look up fertilizers at a busy time, and when crops may be delayed, awaiting their arrival. The experienced cultivator understands all this equally well with the writer, but he is advising the inexperienced, those who inquire of him the why and the wherefore, and to such only, be it understood, is he addressing himself.

Another point of important consideration and of interest to those who design embarking in the business of gardening, whether for market or private gratification, are the implements best adapted for such work.

Implements.—If the operations are designed to

embrace several acres there will be needed a good two-horse steel plow, costing, say ten dollars, for breaking up the soil to a proper depth in spring, and whenever the land is recropped; a light one-horse steel plow, costing five dollars, for drawing open furrows, closing them, earthing up such crops as are benefited by such culture; a harrow, best of iron, as it is lighter than wood; an Iron Age cultivator, with a full set of movable teeth, price three dollars, for pulverizing the soil between drilled crops; a clod crusher, or leveler, readily made of three boards nailed together to form a triangle, to be drawn from either angle; a seed drill, the Matthews or the Model, costing six to eight dollars, both being used on Bloomsdale with satisfaction; or, still better, a Keeler seed drill, price $9.00, which will sow continuous rows, or drop the seed in hills, from ten to thirty-six inches; a Lees wheel hoe costing five dollars; a full set of hoes of various sizes and shapes for side scraping and cross cutting. With these simple implements nearly all the necessary appliances will be at command; others, if needful, may be procured at the hardware stores.

Crates.—The boxes and baskets in which garden products are to be transported to market, are of great importance; for it is self-evident, unless proper precaution be taken, perishable articles may reach their destination so badly damaged as not to be worth the freight.

For strawberries, blackberries and raspberries, very light boxes are manufactured by parties who make a business of it, and sell them at low prices. Some of these are made at so slight a cost as to be given away to the purchaser of the fruit; others are expected to be returned to the commission merchant, who, in turn, dispatches them to the grower from whom they came. Others are made with a view to greater ventilation, and that is of special importance when the point of shipment is distant from market. Peas, beans, cucumbers, can be shipped in ventilated one bushel baskets made for such purposes.

Potatoes usually reach the Northern markets from the South packed in second-hand flour barrels, but it is questionable whether it would not pay to put them up, especially those barely ripe enough to ship, in half barrel or one bushel pea baskets, so as better to adapt the quantity to family wants. But few private persons wish to buy a whole barrel of rare-ripe potatoes, but many families could consume a bushel before they would grow stale, which immature ones are liable to do. Thus, with smaller packages, a direct domestic market could be formed for vast quantities, and not, as now, have the sale confined to provision stores and other retail dealers, each party, through whose hands they pass, adding a profit until they reach so high a price as to deter purchasers from buying liberally.

Pea baskets are gotten up of thin stuff, slatted on all sides, to admit air. There are sometimes rims, or projections, so as to obviate compact storage of the baskets while in transportation, thus securing a sure circulation of air.

Large quantities of potatoes reached the Northern market in former years from Ireland, put up in cylindrical wicker-work hampers, and they came in excellent condition, and it is probable such hampers could be made in the South very cheaply. Oranges and lemons from Florida might also reach the North in the same form, as there are thousands of families who would buy a small hamper of fruit, who now purchase only a dozen at a time. It is not simply the interest of the producer to transport his crop in market, but to do so in a form that will entice customers, by giving them the least possible trouble and inconvenience when supplying their wants. The writer is merely throwing out hints, practical minds will work out the problems themselves.

There may be some people with but little experience in tillage, who imagine the conduct of a farm or garden is like that of a manufactory, where the amplification and extension of the business is only limited by the capital at command; and when they hear of certain large sums being realized from a small plot of ground, argue that the same ratio of profit may be extended over an indefinite area; this is a great mistake, as they are positively certain to realize, if they undertake to prove their theory; and hence we recommend all readers who incline to start in the enterprise herein discussed, to feel their way. One season's experience may enlarge their confidence, or it may teach them without serious loss, that either they or their locations are unfitted to the business. Undoubtedly the greater profit will be found in doing a little well, rather than in imperfect efforts to accomplish more than the facilities at hand warrant one to undertake.

CHAPTER II.

Location and Soils.

As a rule, the best exposure is a gentle slope to the south, but in hilly countries such cannot always be obtained, and good gardens are often seen facing to every point of the compass. The site, face which way it may, should preferably be an even plane, be it level or sloping; that is to say, a table-like surface, without dish-like hollows, on the one hand, or knolls, on the other; but even an inability to meet these latter conditions need not deter an active worker, for frequently the best gardens are met with in localities anything but corresponding to the requirements of theory.

As sunlight is the great factor, in the growth of vegetables, too much attention cannot be given to affording uninterrupted access for every ray of sun to the growing crops, hence no houses, barns, sheds, fences or trees, should be allowed to cast shadows at any time upon the garden surface; and trees, even so located as not to cast a shadow on the crop, may be robbing them both of their moisture and fertility by their wide-reaching roots, which should be cut off by sinking a deep trench between them and the garden.

Soils.—The soil may be anything but brick clay, theoretically a light sandy loam is best, but here, again, astonishing results are often obtained on forbidding soils; for instance, on sticky red clays and sands, the latter seemingly no better than those of the seashore. No soil should be considered entirely bad until it has been proven so.

So much of success or failure in garden operations depends upon the natural character of soil, that the composition of each field of a farm should be closely observed, if not in the scientific view of geological formation and chemical composition, then in the more ordinary view of the mechanical conditions, as respects texture, weight, porosity, adhesiveness and aeration.

Soils may be divided into three divisions, as respects their origin:

1st. Sedimentary—A soil formed entirely out of the local rocks.

2d. Drift—Soils formed out of divers materials, irregularly mixed and deposited without stratification.

3d. Alluvial—A soil of flood deposit by water, the finer particles being on the top.

This soil is the only one, as a rule, of any agricultural value, and it may be said to be derived from broken, pulverized, decomposed rock brought by water from many and far distant parts and deposited in layers, the heavier being at the bottom and the lighter at the top. An alluvial soil may be divided into four distinct classes:

1st. Gravelly—So styled from the abundance of small stones or pebbles of granite, slate, feldspar and limestone.

2d. Sandy—So styled from its composition of small grains of rock. Coarse sands are generally unprofitable, while finer sands are more fertile.

3d. Loamy—So styled as being between the porosity of sand, and the tenacity of clay.

4th. Clayey—So styled from its fineness of texture and retentive power of water. A soil drying and cracking under the effects of hot sun.

A soil, to be fertile, must contain a sufficient quantity of the ash ingredients of the plants to be cultivated, and these must be in such soluble condition as to be taken up by the growing plants. Soils once fertile are said to be exhausted when deprived of such food as is required for plant nutrition, but rest and meliorating treatment will, in time, restore such soils to a fertile condition.

Drainage.

A soil has good drainage when it is of such composition that the rain filters away without flooding the surface, and when, in time of drouth, the evil effects are lessened by the ability of the soil particles to absorb moisture from the air and raise it from the subsoil.

A soil, to be adapted to gardening purposes, must have fair drainage, either natural or artificial, and it is the wisest course to select land naturally possessing these desirable conditions, as the construction of artificial drains is an expensive operation, often doubling the original cost of the land.

Good drainage, like tillage, has a vitalizing effect, admitting of the entry of air and the deposition of its oxygen, carbon and nitrogen; it also warms the soils, while poorly drained land, by the course of evaporation, becomes cold. By deepening the soil, we make it tillable soon after rain, early in the spring, and prevent it from becoming sour, hastening the chemical actions so necessary in promoting the growth of crops.

Tillage and Cultivation.

These operations, often spoken of as the same process, are distinct operations, tillage being the breaking and pulverizing of the soil, a preparation of a seed bed, the work preparatory to the sowing of seed. Cultivation is that work done after the germination of the seed, with the view of developing a rapid growth of the plant, and, incidentally, the suppression of weeds.

In tillage, the ground is broken by plow, spade, or other implement, with a view of dividing the particles of earth and increasing the internal superfices of the soil, for the purpose of holding moisture and absorbing nutritive principles from the air. Tillage is necessary on land of any character, and the more tillage the better the results, for delicate roots cannot take up nourishment as well amid a rough, cloddy, undisintegrated soil, as crops in close contact with a soil well pulverized, which affords, within a limited area, a greater percentage of available air, moisture, organic and inorganic matter.

Tillage is best performed with a spade, but as this is a slow, expensive, and exceedingly laborious process, digging can only be pursued in small gardens. On tracts of an area of one-eighth of an acre and over, the plow, in this country, becomes a necessity, and this implement has now been lightened and perfected so as to do the work almost equal to digging itself. Plowing twice over always pays, three plowings is said to be equal to one manuring. A garden soil may hold plant food enough for five crops, but be practically barren if the fertilizing materials are locked up in impenetrable clods. In tillage, the plow is followed by the harrow, the clod crusher and the roller. Frost is one of the best pulverizers, and it is a well recognized fact that we generally have poor summer crops succeeding mild winters, a consequence of a want of frost action on the soil.

Cultivation is the breaking and working of the soil whilst the crop is growing; the tillage had previously loosened and divided the particles of soil, but during that period of time between the cessation of tillage and the germination and vegetation of the plant the soil, in part, reverts to its more natural solidity, and it is then that cultivation comes in, as an endeavor to retain that friability so necessary to the extension of the roots and their ready nutrition; thus, tillage must always be supplemented by cultivation. To cultivate a crop means to pursue that course with the soil which hastens the development of the plants, and incidentally with this comes in the destruction of weeds, which, allowed to grow, starve the sown plants by robbing them of nutriment. Labor given to tillage, except preparation for broadcast crops, will be, to a large extent, wasted, unless supplemented by such culture of the growing crop as will preserve the earth in a loose and fresh condition. Jethro Tull, a well known agricultural writer, many years ago said, "Tillage is manure."

CHAPTER III.

THE SCIENCE OF GARDENING.

Gardening, as pursued in its higher sense, is both an art and a science. It has arrived at this estate by slow gradations, compared with the development of many other pursuits, but that is consequent upon its complex nature. The development of a knowledge of geology, chemistry, meteorology, vegetable physiology and botany, indeed, something from all branches of human knowledge, has gone to perfect the science of agriculture and horticulture; pursuits affording as wide a range of research in their ramifications as any subject engaging the mind of man, and fully as important in their results. Agriculture, though practiced in early days without any correct knowledge of cause and effect, was always held in high esteem. Columella, contemporary with Virgil, wrote, "The art of husbandry is so necessary for the support of human life, and the comfortable subsistence and happiness of mankind have so great a dependence upon it, that the wisest men in all ages have ascribed its origin to God, as the inventor and ordainer of it, and the wisest of civilized nations, who have best understood their true interests, have always endeavored to promote and improve it, and have never failed to acknowledge and honor, as public benefactors, all such as have contributed anything towards the same." In colonial days our forefathers were almost entirely dependent upon agriculture. Washington, in his agricultural correspondence with Sir John Sinclair, wrote, "It will not be doubted that, in reference either to individuals or to national welfare, agriculture is of primary importance." Webster, of our own generation, wrote, "Agriculture feeds us, to a great extent, clothes us; without it we could not have manufacturers, and we should not have commerce. These all stand in a cluster, the largest in the center, and that largest is agriculture." Agriculture is, indeed, the most fruitful source of the riches of a country, and of the welfare of its inhabitants, and only as the state of agriculture is more or less flourishing can we judge of the progress of a people.

Gardening, which is agriculture upon circumscribed areas, has ever shared with the latter the esteem of mankind. Socrates said, "It is the source of health, strength, plenty, riches and honest pleasure; and an eminent English writer said, "It is amid its scenes and pursuits that life flows pure, the heart more calmly beats."

Agriculture refers to the tillage of the earth over broad fields, as for the raising of cereals, grass or tubers. Gardening, on the other hand, refers to the culture of small inclosed areas. This application of the latter term was quite correct originally, but it is now common for mere vegetable gardens to equal the area of ordinary grain and grass farms, requiring, in their cultivation, a degree of skill and an amount of activity, implements and labor, exceeding that expended upon large farms.

Gardening again differs from farming in the range of varieties cultivated. The farmer may devote his acres to those crops to which his land is adapted, but the gardener is expected to grow the entire list of vegetables, without reference to the composition of the soil. Such cultivation, to be successful, must be, to some extent, scientific. The cultivator must possess a knowledge of the facts and principles which underlie his art, or he will certainly fail.

Viewed in the light of the present age, how ridiculous the directions of the ancients appear! Take Virgil's Georgics, for instance; he, the prince of Latin poets, possessing at once the highest intelligence of his day, experience as a husbandman, and with the stimulus of a royal commission to revive the decaying spirit of husbandry by the insinuating charms of poetry; how crude his teachings pertaining to the laws governing the development of nature in the vegetable and animal kingdoms! Charming to read, even now, and correct still in many practices, yet we are continually jarred by directions the opposite of scientific teaching and experience. The ancients were ignorant of vegetable physiology. Virgil, Pliny and Columella taught that any cion might be grafted on any stock; Pliny mentions the effect of grafting the vine on the elm, and other ridiculous unions. Notwithstanding the numerous superstitions of the Romans, they had acquired many facts pertaining to husbandry; they pruned, watered, fenced, forced, and retarded blossoms and fruit much as we do. Cato, in the second century before the Christian era, writing upon agriculture, said, "What is good tillage? First, to plow; second, to plow; third, to manure. The other part of tillage is to sow plentifully, to choose your seed cautiously, and to remove as many weeds as possible in the season." Thus, it will be perceived, quite a practical view of agriculture was taken two thousand years ago.

Despite the teachings of the ancients, agriculture has for centuries been weighed down by ignorance, prejudice and imperfect action. The force of custom in every country has held the farmer in chains; and such still is, alas, too often the case, even in this land of progress. But to what better pursuit can an able mind turn than to agriculture? Without it men would live wandering lives, disputing with each other for the possession of such animals as they could catch, and for the spontaneous fruits of the earth. Without agriculture there would be no bond of security or love of country; it is, in all countries, the purest source of public prosperity.

One of the greatest of all the sources of enjoyment resulting from the possession of a garden, is the endless variety which it affords, both in the processes of vegetation as it goes forward to maturity, dormancy, or decay, and in the almost innumerable kinds of plants which may be raised, even in the smallest garden. Add to it a small greenhouse, what a source of pleasure and instruction does it not hold out to the amateur? Exactly in proportion as the outdoor work becomes less urgent the indoor operations become more numerous. The amusements and the products which a small glass house affords in the hands of an expert or an ingenious amateur are almost without end. Labor in dealing with inanimate objects has not that enticement and recreation about it which is ever present to him who, aiding nature, witnesses the results of daily toil in living plants changing their forms and colors day by day. Thus, there is a deal of enjoyment to be derived from the different operations of gardening, independently altogether of the health resulting from the exercise.

Investigation into any one of the principles of vegetable growth will develop another, and they, in time, will be found so intimately connected with all the allied branches of natural science as to create a desire for further knowledge of what before were mysteries, but which the intelligence of the present age has developed into science. A well-cultivated garden will awaken inquiry, and start trains of thought and study which otherwise would not be pursued. The close observer will desire to make microscopic observations of the germination of plants, of the growth of fungi, of insect life; and here we pause, for there is opened a volume of nature new to most men, and a source of unexpected pleasure. At the beginning of this century any investigation into the agency of insects, for good or evil, in connection with vegetation, was scarcely considered as belonging to gardening; their eggs passed unnoticed, and the ravages of the larvæ were looked upon frequently as atmospheric blights beyond control. Now the entomologist is consulted every day by the agriculturist and gardener, and no section of the museum of the United States Department of Agriculture is more interesting than that devoted to entomology. Countries of temperate climates in an undeveloped condition support a limited number of species of insect life, and they are generally harmless to vegetation, but, under culture, conditions favorable to their increase are presented. One of these conditions is the wanton destruction of birds, after which follow the myriad tribes of insects which feed upon vegetation; species not alone native to the country, but brought in the course of commerce from all parts of the world. For example, the Hessian fly is supposed to have been brought here in the straw used by the Hessian troops during the Revolution. The cabbage butterfly was brought first into Montreal in cases of crockery from Holland. In ten or twelve years it has extended from the St. Lawrence to the Rio Grande.

The intelligent culturist will be brought to notice the effect of various forms of potash, nitrogen and lime; he will gradually be drawn into geological research, for he must study the peculiar features of the soil. Finally, he will find that the birds are his co-partners in the garden, and the common tomtit or sparrow will no longer be looked upon with a careless eye by reason of his dull colors, but each one welcomed as the destroyer of millions of injurious insects. Even so the bat, ugly and of nocturnal habit, will no longer be driven away or looked upon with disgust, but regarded as a most useful ally. Of what does gardening consist? Of obtaining from the earth vegetables and fruits for man and domestic animals; and the perfection of the art is to obtain the greatest possible product at the least possible expense. From the earliest times gardening has advanced, and receiving always the first attention, it has, in each succeeding generation, become more perfect than in the one preceding.

The development of field and garden culture to its present condition is the result of the union of theory and practice. The greatest expansion has been in a chemical and physiological point of view, and this development, strange as it may seem, dates back not farther than forty years. Agriculture and horticulture before that time may be said to have been conducted under a Virgilian system; cultivators adhering more to blind custom than to reason. In the year 1795 the first book in English upon the relations of agriculture and chemistry was published, and, though containing some truth, its teachings are ridiculous under the light of the present day.

The first accurate analyses of a vegetable was not made till the year 1810, and so late as 1838 the Gottingen Academy offered a prize for a satisfactory solution of the question whether the ingredients of the ashes are essential to vegetable growth. The last forty years have placed agriculture upon a scientific foundation, and the strides of development have been wonderful. The investigations of all scientific men, in their particular pursuits, have served to dispel ancient theories and develop the intricate system of germination, subsistence and growth.

It is, fortunately, the case that every soil holds more or less of the inorganic parts essential to vegetable growth. They may be briefly enumerated as sulphates, phosphates, nitrates, chlorides and carbonates of potash, lime, magnesia, iron and ammonia. Those ingredients that are deficient in quantity can be readily added by the application of stable manure, which contains everything desirable, or by specific application of the constituent wanting. The time has come when every farmer must possess some knowledge of natural history; he must prepare himself, if he expects to follow his pursuit successfully, as much as does the mechanic or the professional man. Why should not the national government establish at frontier army posts agricultural experiment stations? This nation is eminently agricultural, and it is within the province of the government to develop its resources in every practical way.

The war department and the agricultural, working in connection, could, in a few years, establish a series of experiment stations, at once of national importance and of hygienic advantage to each garrison. A post garden is practicable at any military station; of course, under so great a variety of conditions as presented to the soldiers of an army, each garden would differ from the other in some particulars; some upon mountain slopes, others in valleys, on plains both fertile and arid; all influenced by meteorological conditions of widely different effect. Such gardens would have to conform to circumstances, and the more difficult these circumstances may be to surmount, the more pleasure in the results, both in a gastronomic and scientific view.

In Europe they do some things better than we, notwithstanding our boasted practicability, and foremost among their advances is that of public instruction. To-day, in Austria and Sweden, there are many thousands of public schools having gardens attached, where are taught botany, vegetable physiology, and sometimes the whole range of science and art so necessary to a thorough understanding of vegetable growth and development.

Sweden alone possesses two thousand public school-gardens, and there, as in Austria, the system has become so popular that all new school buildings have one room set apart as a school-garden room, where are assembled herbariums, works on agriculture, geology, agricultural chemistry and physiology, and apparatus used by the teachers in their lectures upon plant-life. The public school law passed in Austria in 1869, provided that "In every school a gymnastic ground, a garden for the teacher, according to the circumstances of the community, and a place for the purposes of agricultural experiment be created." The school inspectors of each district are instructed "To see to it that in the country schools school-gardens shall be provided for agricultural instruction in all that relates to the soil, and that the teacher shall make himself skillful in such instruction." The general law declares, "Instruction in natural history is indispensable to suitably established school-gardens. The teachers must, therefore, be in a condition to conduct them." Contrast this thoughtful care with the system, or rather, want of system, for the finer instruction of the mind pursued in the public schools of our rural districts! The time will come when, in this country, as in Europe, more practiced attention must be paid to the practical instruction of the masses in our country districts than now; our boasted public school system, though not retrograding in our cities, has, in the country districts, been far outstripped by that of Germany, Sweden and Scotland, where technical education is now given, fitting the pupils, as men and women, to deal with the affairs of agricultural life.

CHAPTER IV.

CHEMISTRY OF THE GARDEN.

The chemistry of the garden is that science which attempts to define the action of plants upon the chemical constituents of the soil and air; consequently includes the studies of garden geology, the nature of minerals composing the soil, vegetable physiology and plant nutrition, each indicating how the chemical substances are made use of by the vegetable world. The subject of agricultural chemistry is a voluminous and intricate one, and only a very brief reference can be made to it here. Nothing more can be here attempted, than to lead the reader to desire for further information, obtainable from the writings and reports of men like Lawes and Gilbert, of England, Samuel W. Johnson, and others, of this country. All garden and farm plants may, as respects their food, be divided into three classes:

First:—Those requiring an excess of potash, as peas, beans, potatoes, clover, flax.

Second:—Those requiring much nitrogen, as beets, cabbage, oats, wheat, barley and hemp.

Third:—Those requiring large amounts of phosphoric acid, as radish, turnip and corn.

Plants draw some food from the air by their leaves, but most from the earth by their roots. The composition of the air is quite constant, but the character of the soil is exceedingly variable, and crops grown continuously upon a soil draw out one or more of its nutritive principles; consequently, it can only be reinvigorated by returning to it those elements removed in the crops.

CHEMISTRY OF THE GARDEN.

In general, the method of maintaining fertility of soils is by the application of stable or barnyard manure, which may be termed the king of manures, as it can be produced upon every farm, and contains, when good, all the ingredients needed to make a complete and assimilable manure. Most prominent among these ingredients are nitrogen compounds, phosphate of lime, potash and lime. All soils, however, do not need the addition of all four agents; nitrogenous fertilizers are often not needed for peas, beans and clover, leguminous crops. The nitrogenized matter, on the other hand, is often applied to wheat, barley, oats, beets, turnips, and it may be said to be necessary to every crop.

The potash, the active principle of wood ashes, is a suitable fertilizer for peas, beans, clover, flax and potatoes. The phosphate of lime is largely drawn upon by corn, turnip and radish. The chief supply, in a commercial way, is from bones which contain phosphate of lime, carbonate of lime, a little gelatine, albumen and oil.

The lime, ordinarily in the form of carbonate or sulphate, is not so pronounced in its effects, but lime must always be present to produce the best results. The question may occur, where can these concentrated ingredients for the manufacture of a complete manure be obtained; and we meet the query by saying, assimilable nitrogen may be had, to the extent of twenty per cent., in sulphate of ammonia, fifteen per cent. in nitrate of soda, fourteen per cent. in nitrate of potassa, or in dried blood or flesh from slaughter houses or fish factories. These nitrates, preferably that of potassa, are best for vegetables, especially root crops; the sulphates for the cereals. Phosphate of lime can be had, to the extent of fifty per cent., in bone dust, seventy per cent. in bone ashes and bone black, and in superphosphate of lime, which is phosphate of lime treated with sulphuric acid, and which, when properly done, should contain forty per cent. of soluble phosphate.

Potash is contained in wood ashes, but is obtainable in larger quantities in nitrate of potassa, commonly known as saltpeter, which salt should contain forty-five per cent. potash, with the valuable addition of fourteen per cent. of nitrogen. Lime is found chiefly in the carbonate of lime, as chalk or limestone, and in the sulphate of lime, as gypsum or plaster of paris. The sulphate is best, as most soluble. The average prices of these four manurial substances named are :

 Bone phosphate of lime.............1½ cents per pound
 Nitrate of potassa....................6½ " " "
 Nitrate of soda.......................2½ " " "
 Sulphate of ammonia.................3½ " " "
 Sulphate of lime..................... ½ " " "

Bone phosphate varies in commercial value just as it is derived from native phosphates, such as South Carolina or Florida rock, or from animal raw bones. It is, therefore, difficult to fix a value for bone phosphate of lime.

Application of Chemical Manures.—Chemical manures should be distributed as regularly as possible, hence the work cannot be done on a windy day. If time permits, it is well to double the bulk by a mixture of dampened loam, and this addition to the bulk insures a more even distribution. In a general way, we recommend the following application to the crops indicated. For beans, carrots, cucumbers and general garden culture,

 Acid, bone phosphate of lime...........300 pounds
 Nitrate of potassa......................100 "
 Nitrate of soda.........................150 "
 Sulphate of lime.......................150 "
  Costing about sixteen dollars.

For potatoes we recommend :

 Acid, bone phosphate of lime...........250 pounds
 Nitrate of potassa......................150 "
 Sulphate of lime.......................150 "
  Costing about fifteen dollars.

For turnips, ruta baga, corn, sorghum:

    Acid, bone phosphate of lime...........300 pounds
    Nitrate of potassa........................100 "
    Sulphate of lime..........................200 "
        Costing about thirteen dollars.

For beans, peas and clover:

    Acid, bone phosphate of lime...........200 pounds
    Nitrate of potassa........................150 "
    Sulphate of lime..........................200 "
        Costing about fourteen dollars.

For wheat, barley, oats and pasture:

    Acid phosphate of lime..................100 pounds
    Nitrate of potassa........................100 "
    Sulphate of ammonia....................100 "
    Sulphate of lime..........................100 "
        Costing about twelve dollars.

The unexampled collection of wheats shown by Landreth & Son at the Centennial International Exhibition of 1876, were grown on Bloomsdale Farm, fertilized by a preparation made after the last named prescription.

The writer has said stable manure is king, but it cannot always be obtained in quantity, nor at the desired periods; failing to obtain it for present use, we recommend chemical manures, which, used in seasons not too dry, may do equally well at less cost; but if time permits, *green* manures will be found the cheapest.

Nitrogenized matter in the soil is absolutely necessary to the growth of vigorous crops, and the fact cannot be too strongly impressed on every gardener that nitrogen and phosphoric acid are the leading manurial additions required, and a cheap and efficient method of application should occupy his constant attention. Nitrogen, in the form of atmospheric ammonia, is largely obtained by plants through their leaves, but to an equally large extent does the soil get it by absorption, and, if covered, it holds it, and in this simple fact is one of the secrets of *green* manuring. Any cover, whether of boards, hay, straw, or uncut grass, renders the soil quite as fertile by the retention of nitrogen as by the direct value of the constituent parts of the hay, straw, or green matter upon the surface.

That the soil becomes of higher fertility when covered by matter, inert or otherwise, so that the air is not excluded, cannot be denied. A case is known to the writer where a remarkable fertility was shown by a soil which had been covered two years by a board floor on the surface of an open field, the explanation being that the soil daily absorbs ammonia from the air, from rain, dew, and decay of organic matter, while, on the other hand, if not covered, these absorptions are as rapidly lost by volatilization.

Of course, the most natural and cheapest covering for the soil is a green crop, and if the green manuring is to be done between spring and autumn, experience points to corn as the best crop, two half-grown crops being better than one allowed to reach such a development as to be difficult to plow under, the first crop being planted at the usual season, and the second sixty to seventy days subsequently, the latter crop being plowed under after frost checks its growth.

On Bloomsdale Farm, this system has been pursued with profit, but, better still, rye sown in the October following the corn. Rye has proved to be the best green manure sown in October or November, and, when properly put in, will produce a sponge-like mat of from four to five tons of root fibers and fifteen to sixteen tons of green herbage to turn under in April or May, and early enough, except in the far South, for crops of potatoes, onions, melons and corn. Rye, grown during autumn and winter, only occupies the ground during a season when no other crop except wheat would be standing out, and it covers the soil during a critical period. The cost of a green crop of rye should not be over four dollars to the acre, say one dollar for seed, one and a half dollars for the preparation of the land, one and a half dollars for turning under.

Four crops of green manure can be turned down in seventeen months, by seeding rye in October, corn in April, a second crop of corn in July, and rye again in October, to be plowed under in April. This rotation will surprise the experimenter, who will see his soil made fertile, friable, and in general vigor far beyond its previous condition, all due to the valuable component parts of the vegetable matter plowed under, and to the absorption and retention of nitrogen by the soil consequent upon the extended covering of the surface. From the earliest agricultural records green manuring has been practiced, and whole districts of country in Europe have been rendered fertile by such practice. A large district in Germany, once a barren, is now most fertile, all due to the use of the lupine, which plant, however, does not offer such good results under the hot sun of the American climate.

CHAPTER V.

Stable Manure, Compost and Commercial Fertilizers.

Stable manure of good quality cannot be obtained in every locality, and it may be practical to consider, first, how poor stable manure can be improved, and, secondly, how a poor grade may be mixed with other materials to form a compost. Stable manure, in its general designation, indicates all the refuse from the stall and barnyard, and, consequently, includes good, bad and indifferent. Of course, the prominent material in stable manure is straw of wheat, rye, oats or barley, with smaller proportions of hay or fodder—these mixed with the droppings and urine of cattle. The quality varies with the proportion, in the mass, of the excretion of animals. Stable manure is best applied when well broken up by fermentation. If not decayed but in long strawy condition, or otherwise green condition, it should be piled till fermentation sets in to reduce it, or it should be composted.

In strong fermented stable manure there is often developed an immense number of insect larva, the rich mass attracting the mature insects, in which they lay their eggs; which dung also frequently developes many varieties of fungous growth, ready to effect lodgment on such crops as may be naturally fitted for their further development. The best stable manure is that exclusively from the stables of well fed horses, as such is composed only of hay, straw, urine and horse dung, digested and half digested food of forage and grass, the richer the food given to the horse the better the excrement. This, as taken from the stalls, is known as fresh manure, and is slow in fertilizing action. To render it active agriculturally it must be piled, that fermentation may proceed to break down the component parts and bring them into condition to afford quick nutrition to growing plants. The fresh manure is suitable for application in winter, or to a crop requiring a slow fertilization, but to spring and autumn crops in the garden it is too slow, consequently if we use stable manure to develop an early effect it must be rotten, or short, as it is termed.

The value of stable manure, of course, varies in every locality. Farmers in New York, Pennsylvania and Delaware pay for stable manure delivered on railroad cars eighty to one hundred miles out from the city, from New York and Philadelphia, $2.00 per ton including freight. The cleanings from stalls should be piled as taken out, and this is best done under a shed, as too frequent rains wash out a portion of the most soluble ingredients, though a limited amount of water must be present in the pile all the time or the manure will burn or grow white within the pile, and its value be injured as much as if subjected to too much water; thus, as in all things, there is a happy medium. Stable manure of indifferent quality, strawy, not rich in dung, containing little digested or half-digested grain, not putrefactive, may be started into more rapid fermentation by densely piling it, and, as it is piled, watering it with a fermenting solution.

Fermenting Lye.—The solution, or lye, may be compared to horse urine, and will exert the same effect in starting a like fermentation. To every ton of crude stable manure apply the lye as the manure is corded up in ten inch layers. The ingredients necessary to make the lye to test a ton of crude stable manure need not cost more than one dollar, and are: Two bushels of pulverized quicklime, one bushel of land plaster, one-fourth bushel of common refuse salt, three pounds of saltpeter, three pounds of muriatic acid, stirred in with three barrels of rich barnyard water. The lye can be made in oil or whisky barrels, and, after making, should stand several hours before application. Barnyard water, the drainage from manure, is almost as important as the solid parts, as, to a considerable extent, it is a diluted solution of urine, the very agent which the preparation is intended to represent in its action. The larger the bulk the more perfect will be the action of the lye.

Compost.—Compost, in an agricultural sense, is understood to be a compounded manure of the varied collections of the garden, as crude stable manure, swamp mud, leaves, weeds, swamp grass, sea grass, old sods, king crabs, jelly fish, fresh or salt fish, tobacco stems, pumice from cider mills, waste wool, refuse from soap factories, tallow waste from slaughter houses, and any vegetable or animal product. The compost pile, if made of good materials, should be a well disintegrated mass of equal quality, throughout, in fertilizing substances, in ready condition for quick assimilation by plants. The process of fermentation and disintegration may be hastened in compost piles by the same application of a fermenting solution as described for coarse stable manure.

For one ton of compost we recommend two bushels of powdered quicklime, one bushel of land plaster, one-half bushel of refuse salt, ten pounds of saltpeter, ten pounds of muriatic acid, all mixed in three barrels of barnyard water. This mixture, costing about two dollars and a half, will weigh about thirteen hundred pounds, and, if further diluted, as would be advisable, the ton of compost, when treated, will weigh two tons. In the application of the lye, the compost should be worked, and packed up in a square, round, or other compact form, applying the solution to every layer of five or six inches, that the lye may dampen every portion.

Commercial Fertilizers.

A commercial fertilizer is an article of concentrated strength, and adapted to transportation, storage and easy application. These fertilizers may be divided into three classes. First, articles found in natural deposits, as Peruvian guano or Chili saltpeter. Second, articles resulting from a manufacture or process, as fish chum from the oil works, dried blood from the slaughter house, graves from tallow works, or odorless phosphate from the basic process of making Bessemer steel. Third, compounded materials, those requiring manufacture, as superphosphate, and the various combinations of potash and soda. While commercial manures were used in England fifty years ago, they did not become common in the United States until about 1844, when Peruvian guano was introduced, and this, then as now (more so then than now), was a complete manure, the early shipments sometimes containing as much nitrogen as phosphoric acid, and also a large percentage of potash.

The chief merit of Peruvian guano is due to the fact that it has been accumulated in a region where it never rains, as upon the Chincha Islands, or only occasionally upon the Labos Islands, and though fifty per cent. of Peruvian guano is soluble in water it thus remained intact, and did so remain for ages, until the deposits, in some places, accumulated to one hundred feet in thickness, the droppings from birds, and other materials, all derived from the weeds and fish of the sea. There are other bird guanos collected from various islands in other seas, but having been subjected to rains, have lost most of their nitrogen and potash, the phosphoric acid being retained; these have been termed phosphatic guanos, while the Chilian grades are termed nitrogenous guanos. The natural sources of phosphoric acid are the rock phosphate, extensively used by the superphosphate manufacturers, large quantities being brought from the island of Navassa, near St. Domingo, and from the South Carolina and Florida phosphate beds. The artificial sources of supply are the vast plains of South America, from whence have been collected and exported the bones of innumerable herds of cattle slain for their hides, and millions of others dying from natural causes, during the past one hundred and fifty years.

Potash, used commercially as a fertilizer, was at first derived from wood ashes, and often from feldspar, and the supply was long insufficient; but about 1860 the salt miners of Prussia discovered large deposits of potash salts, which have since been the main supply for the manufacture of fertilizers the world over, the damaging chloride of magnesium being first removed. These Prussian mines are vast deposits of saline matter, evidently crystalized out of sea water. Before crude salts can be advantageously sold and transported they have to go through a course of preparation which, according to the nature of the deposit and the process, develops sulphate of potash and muriate of potash.

Nitrogen, as an article of commerce, has been obtained in large quantities from Peru and Chili, in the form of Chili saltpeter, found in the interior of those countries in vast quantities, sometimes many feet in thickness. As much as four million tons have been exported annually, but the Peruvian government has now reserved these deposits for domestic use. Of course, there are other sources of nitrogen, especially in the by-products of manufactures, for example, sulphate of ammonia, from gas works. Animal nitrogen is largely obtained from fish scrap, of which sixty thousand tons are annually produced on the Atlantic coast. Of course, the raw or fresh fish will furnish this same ammonia. The writer has plowed under, on his firm's farms in Lancaster county, Virginia, from seven to nine millions of fish annually; the fish being menhaden, a species slightly smaller than herring. Cracklings from the tallow works, dried blood and tankage from slaughter houses, are valuable sources of supply for agricultural nitrogen.

By the introduction of commercial fertilizers farm operations have been freed from the restrictions and limitations imposed by the deficient sources of home-made manures, and the intelligent farmer may vastly extend his operations, while the scientific one turns his farm into a factory, where he endeavors, sometimes, with the aid of climatic influences, and sometimes defeated by such influences, to manufacture his products.

The world-wide use of commercial fertilizers has served to establish a standard of agricultural value of all the ingredients, and their high price has stimulated the inquiring gardener to a closer scrutiny into the entire subject, not only of plant nutrition, but as respects human foods. He is thus lifted above the laborious routine of digging, plowing and harrowing, and becomes a student of nature. By the application of commercial manure the gardener has an advantage over the use of stable manure in the avoidance of adding to the stock of weed seed natural to his land, stable manure always containing more or less seeds of grain or weeds. The use of commercial fertilizers, on the other hand, while raising agriculture to a higher level of intellectual thought, has made a large class of farmers indifferent, if, indeed, not strangers, to the old school methods of farm recuperation, a condition much to be regretted.

Commercial fertilizers will always be in demand, and much of the success of our agriculturists depends upon the capital and talent of the manufacture of such manures. A fair amount of confidence can be placed in well made fertilizers, due principally to the enactment of laws by several of the State legislatures requiring from manufacturers sworn statements of analysis, and also to the very critical investigations and comparisons made at the various State experiment stations.

CHAPTER VI.

Sowing Seeds.

In this we refer to the sowing or planting of the seeds of vegetables or flowers in the *open* garden. Every sane man knows that a preparation of the land is necessary, but when and how to make the preparation can only be learned by reading, observation or experience. Experience in the garden, like experience in all matters of life, is the most practical teacher; when and how to dig or plow, when to harrow or rake, to clean the ground, to fertilize, to open trenches, or cast up ridges, whether to drill in long parallel rows, or across narrow beds, all of which operations are preliminary to the actual operations of seeding. The practice of seeding differs on the part of equally capable men; the conditions, the quantity to be grown, and whether for family or market garden, leading to variations in processes.

Much disappointment in the garden often results from ignorant practices, as from unseasonable sowing, as from too deep or too shallow covering, from injudicious selection of varieties, from inefficient thinning out that the plants may have room to properly develop, from want of preparatory tillage and subsequent cultivation. Of course, the amount of seed properly sown to the acre, or to the row, by persons of equal experience, differs as much as does their process of sowing or method of cultivation. It is generally considered, however, that it is unwise to spare the amount of seed, as the difference in cost of a thick seeding, compared with a thin one, amounts to little as compared with the disappointment, and, still greater, the loss resulting from a deficient stand of plants. Ordinarily the quantity of seed to be sown is said to be so many bushels or so many pounds to the acre, but this does not, by any means, indicate to the gardener, who may only have one acre on which to plant all his crops, the amount he should obtain to meet his necessities. It is better, in such cases, to indicate the quantity of seed required to sow one hundred yards of continuous rows, as the gardener, measuring the length of the rows intended to be devoted to various kinds of plants, can calculate exactly how many ounces or quarts he should procure. Such a ready table for reference will be found in the following:

SEEDS REQUIRED FOR A ROW ONE HUNDRED YARDS LONG.

One ounce of cabbage, cauliflower, collards, broccoli, Brussels sprouts, egg-plant, kale, kohl-rabi, pepper, squash, pumpkin, tomato, turnip.

Two ounces of onion, leek, lettuce, endive, parsley, canteloupe.
Three ounces of carrot, cress, celery, chervil, water melon, parsnip, herbs.
Four ounces of cucumbers, nasturtium, rhubarb, salsify, scorzonera.
Five ounces of beet.
Six ounces of radish, spinach.
Eight ounces of corn salad.
Twelve ounces of okra, asparagus.
One pint of field corn.
One quart of sugar corn.
Three quarts of bush beans, peas.

In a country of such diversity of soil and climate as the United States, it is difficult, indeed, impossible, to advise, except in a very general way, as to processes of tillage, seeding and culture. With sixteen hundred and fifty miles of territory north and south, three thousand five hundred miles east to west, a surface level in some places with the sea, in others four to eight thousand feet elevation, some districts having an annual rainfall of ten to twenty inches, others of one hundred and twenty inches, soils differing with varying geological formation on two thousand millions of acres, an acreage nearly equal to the entire continent of Europe.

In correspondence the writer accordingly adopts the policy of advising inquirers to observe the practice of successful gardeners in their respective localities, and follow that system as a far safer practice than anything he can advise from experience, necessarily limited to the Middle States. In the Northern and Middle States the average season for open air seeding may be indicated by the blooming of well known trees and shrubs, though seeding may be made with profit, both before and after such periods, as it is a safe rule, in gardening, to divide the risks. For instance, when the *peach* is in bloom sow those seeds which will germinate in cold soil, resist slight frost, as peas, spinach, onion and leek. When the *oak* bursts its leaf buds, sow beet, carrot, celery, lettuce, parsnip, radish, salsify, turnip, tomato. When the *blackberry* is in bloom sow those seeds which will thrive only in warmer soil, as the bean, corn, cucumber, canteloupe, watermelon, pumpkin, squash, okra.

No occupation of business, no occupation of pleasure, affords so much for interesting study, as the growth and treatment of vegetables, and the study of their soils, their fertilizers and tillage. It must be borne in mind, however, that those who would avoid labor should leave gardening alone, because it is a perpetual combat with enemies, rain, drouth, frost, heat, weeds, insects, and the unexpected from every quarter.

CHAPTER VII.

Germination.

The process of germination may be said to cover that period of time from the moment of planting the dry seed to the appearance of the new plant, and continuously on till the young plant, exhausting the food stored in the mother seed, is capable of sustaining itself by attachment to the soil. Very few garden seeds will start at a lower temperature than 50°, many requiring a warmth of 70°. On the other hand, too much heat dries up the germ, few kinds resisting a temperature above 120°. The moist, rapid germination of seeds in general is at a temperature from 70° to 90°. Under low temperature root growth is very slow, while under high temperature the development of roots is far in excess of a counter-balancing leaf development.

Moisture is indispensable to germination, but the amount most favorable varies with different plants; for instance, some seeds will only start when in water. Garden seeds will do best when the land is moist, but not wet; too much moisture causes decay; and they may be divided into two classes, as respects their germination, viz.: Cold soil and warm soil seeds, the first class comprising peas, onions, lettuce, radish and spinach; the second class includes the greater number, sprouting freely by the aid of much solar or artificial heat.

Time for Germination.—The time required in germination greatly varies, dependent upon the species of plant, the age of the seed and the surrounding conditions of soil and atmosphere. Under favorable circumstances, peas, beans and corn should sprout in three days; cabbage, turnip and radish in four days; vine seeds, such as melon, squash and cucumber, in five or six days. Germination, however, does not guarantee vegetation, as seeds showing a germ may never appear above ground if physically weak, if too deeply covered, or if the soil is hardened by rain or heat. As a rule, the depth for covering seeds should be three to four times their diameter.

Rapid Growth Desirable.—The great principle conducive to quick, healthy germination and rapid vegetation is a fine seed bed and good tillage. A rapid growth of garden plants is much to be desired, as they then outstrip the weeds, and, to a degree, get beyond such dangers as floods, grubs and insects, which play havoc with young seedlings, especially those of delicate structure. Healthy, uniform germination requires warmth, moisture, and air, as climatic accessories to a finely pulverized soil, which preserves the moisture longer than rough land. Seeds, on the other hand, sown amid clods and crevices, are, many of them, lost by depth of covering, while the rough surface of such land quickly bakes and cracks and offers shelter to annoying vermin.

Vitality of Seeds.—The time during which vegetable seeds retain their vitality is very variable, dependent, first, upon their chemical composition; second, upon the climatic condition under which they were harvested; third, upon the greater or lesser moisture of the air in which they are stored; and, fourth, upon proper ventilation of the bags or packages. On the southern seaboard, and in the Gulf States, where the air is very moist, at times, perfectly fresh seeds frequently lose their vitality by the end of the first year, while far inland and in dry sections of the country, and especially in high latitudes, they may, with few exceptions, be safely used the second season. The primary cause, however, of difference in period of duration of the growing powers of seed, depends principally upon difference in their chemical composition.

All seed may be divided into two classes, those in which oil predominates, those in which starch predominates; and it is the first which most rapidly change by decomposition, the starchy seeds, with the exception of corn, being least subject to chemical change and most tenacious of life.

Testing Seeds.—When it is desired to determine the vitality of a seed, the test should always be made by counting out lots of one hundred seeds, just as they are, good, bad and indifferent; better still, to take several lots of one hundred seeds of each variety, that one lot may serve to prove the other. In all such cases the experimenter should have a sample of *another lot* of the same variety of seed from a distinct source, of which he already knows the true vitality, this to serve as a proof or standard in estimating the accuracy of the test. The test of vitality may be made in a number of ways, the most reliable, of course, being in earth; sandy loam in broad pots or trays, well placed as respects heat and moisture, or, better still, the seed sown in earth on the benches of a greenhouse.

A second method of testing seeds is by germinating them in flannel cloths suspended over water trays, from which the flannel becomes damp by capillary attraction.

By this process, excepting for egg plant, pepper, and such other seeds as require heat, a higher test can be made than by the earth test, but the flannel test is deceptive, as many seeds will start and show a sprout, while unable to make further growth for want of vital force. Such seeds, under the flannel test, are counted as good, while under the earth test they never would be counted, as they never would appear above the surface, being too weak to force their way through the soil.

A test of somewhat similar character to the flannel test can be made by placing the seeds between two bats of cotton, each one inch thick and three to four inches wide, kept constantly wet and near a stove, or in the sun, that the water may not become cold. Seeds of the oily class, as cabbage, cauliflower and turnips, should have, when first harvested, if gathered under dry conditions, and if well cleaned, an average vitality of eighty to ninety-five per cent. The second year the percentage falls to seventy and eighty per cent; the third year to sixty and seventy per cent., and so on in a declining scale to nothing after seven or eight years.

Carrot, parsley, spinach, or parsnip seeds are much affected by harvest conditions, and as respects cleaning or the separation of the good from the bad, after threshing. The first year they grow from seventy to eighty per cent., the second year fall to fifty and sixty per cent., the third year forty to thirty per cent., and the fourth year may be considered valueless.

Cucumber, canteloupe, squash, pumpkin and watermelon require cautious harvesting and washing to prevent sprouting during the process, and, when well washed and dried, have a vitality the first year of eighty to ninety per cent., the second year seventy to seventy-five per cent., the third year sixty to seventy per cent., decreasing over a period of five or six years.

Pepper, egg plant and okra seed are especially weak in vital force, seldom showing over seventy per cent. of germination the first year, and often not half that the second, and sometimes less. Beet seed containing from three to five germs to the single capsule will often develop three hundred shoots to a hundred seeds, but after a period of four years the percentage of vitality will fall to twenty-five per cent., though the writer has now growing a ten acre crop from a lot of select seed of Bassano beet eight years old. American grown onion and leek seed varies from seventy to ninety per cent. in vitality the first year, falling to about sixty the second year and thirty the third. These seeds of English and French growth, when brought to the United States, seldom have a vitality of two-thirds of the percentage of the American. Frequently the best English leek seed cannot be found to show over twenty-five per cent. Radish, if of American growth, should have a vitality of ninety to ninety-five per cent. the first year, and will diminish ten per cent. for four or five years. Of European growth it seldom has over seventy per cent. vitality the first year, ofttimes not more than fifty per cent., and the second year frequently falling to twenty-five per cent., and sometimes less, by reason of the conditions of excessive moisture under which it is harvested and cured, and the moisture absorbed during the ocean voyage.

Lettuce, endive, celery and tomato being seeds difficult in the separation after threshing of the good from the bad, seldom have a vitality of over eighty per cent. Lettuce and endive, however, are very retentive of germinating quality, falling not more than ten per cent. per annum, annually, for three or four years, after which they decline rapidly to nothing, celery and tomato being least vital.

Peas, well riddled and hand picked, should have a vitality the first year, if harvested in dry weather, of ninety-five per cent., the second year eighty per cent., the third year sixty per cent., after which they will

GERMINATION.

deteriorate so rapidly as to be of no value. Beans are much more liable to injury than peas, ripening during later and less favorable weather for drying, and encased in more succulent pods. Wax pod beans are especially delicate, but when harvested under good conditions and hand picked, should have a vitality of ninety to ninety-five per cent. They, however, deteriorate rapidly, to eighty per cent. the second year, to sixty per cent. the third, and the fourth to twenty per cent.

Corn varies greatly in germinating force, the flint varieties being the most vital, the dent sorts, the gourd seed sorts and the sugar varieties following in the order named. Hard, flinty corn, grown under good conditions, and well cured, should germinate the first year to the extent of ninety per cent., the second year to eighty per cent., and the third year to fifty per cent. Sugar corns, on the other hand, are very delicate, their vitality being affected by the conditions under which they are matured, husked, cured and packed, and, even after seeming hard and dry, they often become damp if kept in bulk or in bags piled up. So delicate are sugar corns that they should never be continuously kept in bags or sacks till the January following the harvest, and often not that early.

There are unauthenticated records of mummy corn from South America having germinated, but the writer doubts the accuracy of the statements. He has an ear of mummy corn from Peru, said to be seven hundred years old, but it is entirely dead, having been subjected, as all other mummy corn has been, to the heating effects of hot pitch and similar mixtures used in embalming. The claim that corn of vital force has been found in the Egyptian tombs is positively false, as small grain was found. Maize was entirely unknown on the Eastern continents before the discovery of America. Credulous tourists visiting the Nile regions can always be accommodated, by obliging native guides, with maize said to be from the tombs, but it is of recent growth.

In making comparisons of the vitality of vegetable seeds, it must always be borne in mind that English, French and German seeds are never as vital as American, consequent upon the excessive humidity of the seed-growing regions abroad and the injurious effects of a sea voyage. The European crops are never ripened in the field as thoroughly as the American, and before and after threshing are never in as bone-dry condition as crops ripened under semi-tropical heat; consequently European seeds do not sprout as quickly, do not develop the same large percentage of vitality, and do not hold what they have so well as seeds of American growth. A low percentage of vitality, either of European or American seeds, does not necessarily indicate age, but, frequently, that the seed was matured under unfavorable circumstances, conditions beyond the power of the seed grower to avoid. No seed grower could undertake to guarantee the vitality of the seed sold by him, for he cannot control the conditions of the sowing as respects nature of soil, preparation of seed bed, previous condition, present manuring, time and manner of seeding, immunity from fleas and larvæ at time of sprouting, conditions of moisture and temperature. The seedsman who guaranteed his seed would either be a fool or a knave.

While vitality is of much importance, it is less so than purity. An apparent want of vitality is often wholly due to some unfavorable condition, as one planter frequently succeeds while another fails with the seed out of the same bag. Again, a low vitality of a newly harvested seed, the result of climatic conditions, is a matter beyond human control, and, occasionally, seed of such defective vitality has to be accepted by both seed grower, merchant and planter. Not so with impurity;

for if seed prove unvital a new purchase can be made, and a new planting follow within a few days; but impure seed is more deceptive, as its very vigor secures the crop, attention and labor to be subsequently found wasted. Of the two evils, unvital seed or impure seed, the first, by all odds, is the least.

CHAPTER VIII.

Transplanting.

Many seeds of garden vegetables, and of nearly all garden flowers, are first sown in beds, to be afterwards transplanted to permanent positions, with the object,

First :—That by their concentration more thorough attention can be given them as respects preparation of seed bed.

Second :—Because the space in which they ultimately stand may be occupied by an immature crop.

Third :—That delicate plants might be lost if sown in permanent positions and subjected to the attacks of insects, or overgrown by weeds.

Fourth :—To save labor, as one thousand small plants in a bed can be cared for at one-tenth the cost of time and money as the same number in open ground.

Fifth :—To induce productiveness, as plants set out from beds to the open ground are checked in their vigor of leaf growth and a clearly indicated disposition developed, in the direction of blooming and early maturity. The beds in which delicate, slow growing vegetable plants are grown may be hotbeds, intermediate beds, cold frames or out door border beds, but from all or any of them the plants must be moved with equal care, for transplanting is an operation so delicate as not only to determine whether a crop be secured or not, but to grade the productiveness and time of maturity. Beets, carrots, parsnips, radish, turnip and all other fleshy tap-rooted plants are best grown on permanent positions, as they do not transplant well, but many fibrous-rooted plants, as cabbage, tomato, egg plant, pepper, lettuce, are most safely started in beds, and really do best after transplanting, as they then are afterward more deeply set in the soil and start off upon fresh tilled land as well as while growing in the bed, giving the gardener ample time to make all desirable arrangements for transplanting, while, on the other hand, if he sowed the seed in permanent position at the same early date he might fail to secure good plants.

The process of transplantation should be performed on soils properly tilled; that is, thoroughly plowed or dug, harrowed or raked, and marked off in rows at proper intervals for hand hoeing, or wider for horse cultivation. While transplantation by thoroughly experienced persons can sometimes be done under unfavorable conditions of soil, it is, as a rule, only safely undertaken when the soil is damp or wet, when the rain is falling, or the air charged with moisture, otherwise the plants may succumb under hot sun or drying winds.

In setting the plants in the row, space should always be allowed between them greater than the extreme diameter of the fully developed plant. For instance, if a certain variety of cabbage will produce a head and outside leaves of a space of fifteen inches, then that variety of plant should be set at eighteen inches; or if one variety of lettuce plant grows twelve inches in diameter and another variety only five inches, they should be set accordingly.

In taking plants from seed beds they should not be pulled up, to the destruction of the rootlets, but lifted with a trowel or similar tool, and when out of the ground should be protected from sun or air, as either influence will dry up those tender fibers upon which depend its earlier or later connection with the soil. The coarse roots may be looked upon as so many anchors; they do not sustain the life of the plant. The plants dug from the seed beds and properly protected, the next operation is to set them, which may be done with a dibble or trowel. The dibble is a long, pointed, cone-shaped tool, which, from its form and rotary motion when used, generally smooths the sides of the hole, both bad features, while a trowel is a digging implement, leaving the soil mellow.

The plants should be set deeper than they originally stood, but as a rule, not deeper than the points of attachment of the lower leaves. None of the root fibers should point upward, be all turned downward, and the more widely spread the better. The soil should be pressed down with the hand or foot after the plant is set, that the earth and rootlets may be brought into intimate contact, otherwise the time required to bring about this contact is so much lost time. It is a good practice to hoe a transplanted crop just as soon as the plants recover from the setting, as hoeing mellows the soil and has a vitalizing effect.

Mulching.—In small gardens the practice of mulching after transplanting is often pursued with marked advantage. This operation is the covering of the soil around freshly set plants, vines, shrubs and trees, with three to four inches in depth of litter of any kind, long manure, dry hay, dried leaves, green grass from the lawn, green weeds from the field or garden, any of them preventing, during dry weather, excessive evaporation from the soil.

Crops well mulched are comparatively free from weeds, and such as do push themselves through it can easily be pulled up, while the moist, mellow condition of the soil under a mulch renders ordinary cultivation unnecessary. Every cultivator not familiar with the merits of mulching should make some experiments, the material always being cheap, indeed, often in the way, and presenting a problem as to its disposition.

CHAPTER IX.

Succession, or the Rotation of Crops.

The gardener, whether an expert or amateur, must, like a general in the field, have a plan of operations upon which to conduct the campaign of the summer, and, while the expert may not commit his plan to paper, the amateur certainly should, otherwise he will more than double the number of the errors which he is sure to commit, plan he ever so well.

Gardening, it is true, is often successfully pursued by seemingly ignorant men, and they truly may be ignorant of literature and polite accomplishments, but they are, nevertheless, specialists, and if successful operators in the advanced system of gardening, may prove themselves to have acquired a technical knowledge which is as much a profession as any other occupation which develops looked for results.

The amateur has everything to learn, and must commit his plans to paper, or he will be certain to run everything into disorder, and, before the season is well started be disposed to give up in despair of ever getting things into order by strawberry time. With a clear, systematically managed garden, his is the envy of all neighbors, while with a weedy and clearly unprofitable one he sets such a bad example that it would have been better he had not attempted anything. The gardener must do a little engineering, he must have a plan of his garden drawn to a scale, say one-third of an inch to the foot, and on three distinct sheets lay out the plans for spring, summer and autumn. As to the nature of these plans, the reader may get some hints from observation of the practice of good market gardeners in his vicinity or elsewhere. Now, presupposing that the spring planting of the private gardener comprises every thing seasonable, the question naturally arises what shall he sow as a succession to his spring planting; for be it clearly understood, it is only by keeping up in the garden a never ceasing course of sowing of seed, gathering of matured crops, and re-sowing on the same ground, without any waste of time, that the garden can be practically made to pay its cost in dollars and cents. With a less intense system of administration and culture it may pay well, in the pleasure derived from the contemplation of rural subjects and in increased health consequent upon interesting and moderate outdoor labor, but unless the course of rotation is well thought out and practically put into effect each fruit or vegetable will cost double its price in the stores. Of course the climatic location has everything to do with the policy adopted, as in the Gulf States the practice is quite distinct from that of the Carolinas, and in the Carolinas equally distinct from that of the corn and wheat growing districts of the East and West. In fact, in each section of each State distinct policies are pursued as to periods of sowing, and as to choice of varieties.

As an aid to the amateur in the Middle and Western States we will say that peas may be followed by cabbage for early autumn use, also by beans, tomato and celery plants. Onions by kale, turnip and winter radishes. Spring spinach by beans and tomatoes. Spring radishes by cabbage, for early autumn use. Lettuce by beans and tomatoes. Beans by kale, turnip, winter radishes, autumn lettuce and celery. Early carrots by autumn spinach, kale, turnips, winter radishes. Summer squash by kale, turnip, winter radishes. Cucumber by autumn spinach, turnip and winter radishes. Early beets by spinach, kale, turnips and winter radishes. Early sugar corn by a second crop of the same kind or by autumn spinach, beans, tomatoes, celery.

There are some late maturing varieties of garden plants which seldom afford the cultivator an opportunity to sow anything else as a succession; among these are late sugar corns, parsley, parsnip, leek, pumpkin, melons, winter squarsh, tomatoes, okra and peppers.

Thinning Out.

It takes a determined conviction of necessity to thin out young plants in the vegetable or flower garden, that they may have full space to properly extend their growth. Among vegetables of large leaf development, as cabbage, lettuce, spinach and parsley, the space necessary for growth without crowding, may be found by marking round the plant a circle on the ground equal to the diameter of a fully developed specimen, and those plants with large roots, such as beets, radish and turnip, must be allowed room in proportion to their usual size.

Do not hesitate to thin out, no matter how sturdy and attractive the plants may be, for the plant which crowds another is simply a weed. This thinning should be done before the plants be drawn or elongated in their stems or leaves, or they will ever afterward show the injurious effects of crowding. It may be done by cutting out with a hoe or knife of those plants which are not needed elsewhere, or, if considered worth transplanting, they should be carefully dug up, that the finer roots be preserved. No vegetable or flower will properly develop if crowded; certainly one symmetrical plant is worth a dozen sickly ones, not only for market, but in effect.

CHAPTER X.

Garden Insects.

Owing to the depredations of sparrows, blackbirds, chickens, and other feathery thieves, moles and mice underground, squirrels, woodchucks, cats and dogs above ground, the painstaking gardener will find many of his labors frustrated by an innumerable host of enemies coming and going throughout the season. Among these may be included slugs, grubs, cutworms, caterpillars, sap suckers, plant lice, the larva of day butterflies and night moths in various stages of transformation. Some seasons they all appear to be present and combine in an attack to defeat every operation of the gardener. At other times they most graciously absent themselves; but the gardener is never without a sufficient number to keep him well on the defensive.

Insecticides.—The subject of insecticides and traps is one to which is now given much attention, and country stores in every district are all well supplied with preparations and apparatus without number, all offered as the best, however poor.

An unscientific description of a few of the common destructive insects in the garden, with suggested remedies for destroying them, may not be out of place. Insect preventives may be said to be of two forms of application: Steeps, in which the seed, before sowing, is soaked, and dressings, with which the plants are covered. These may again be divided into two classes: Repellants, as gasoline, tar, kerosene, sulphur powder, which act by overcoming the natural odor of plants attractive to certain insects, and poisons, generally arsenical compounds, applied with the direct intent of killing the insect eating the foliage.

In nothing is the saying that "An ounce of prevention is worth a pound of cure," more exemplified than in the advantage derived from destroying flying insects before they deposit their eggs. Every one living in the country is familiar with the habit of night moths and bugs to fly into lamps or other lights, and that the inclination has been used as a means of inviting them to destruction by night fires on the borders of the garden, or by placing in the midst of the garden a large tub of water, over the center of which is placed a square lantern against which the insects fly violently and are precipitated into the water.

Asparagus Beetle.—The asparagus beetle, often called the asparagus fly, is an oblong, hard-bodied, quick motioned insect, about one-third of an inch in length, its head black, its thorax tawny red, and wing-covers blue-black, ornamented with six small yellow spots, appearing in large numbers during the season of asparagus cutting; the soft larvæ, or slugs, are most ravenous destroyers of the cuticle or outer bark of stems, twigs and leaves of the asparagus plant, attacking it from the first peeping sprout in early spring till the plant has reached its full development. These insects, maturing early, develop a new brood in August. Nothing can be done to destroy the asparagus beetle upon the marketable shoots, as mineral poisons would be destructive to human life, and offensive applications would destroy the value of the crop.

On beds not old enough for cutting, and on beds past prime condition, mineral poisons may be used, and none have been found better than Paris green, mixed with forty parts of flour. Sometimes the beetles appear in such numbers and are so voracious that asparagus shoots for market require to be cut when just peeping through the ground, otherwise in a day nothing would remain to be collected.

Asparagus beds past the marketable condition of growth can be dressed advantageously with a solution of a tablespoonful of Paris green in four gallons of water, which will be generally found to kill the slugs. Sometimes effective results ensue by the application of freshly slaked lime while the dew is on them, for the least particle of lime touching the skin of a slug is certain to kill it.

White Grub.—The white grub is the larvæ of the familiar June bug, or, more correctly, May beetle, which, in the early spring months, enters dwellings in the evening, swarming about the lights, buzzing loudly and violently, knocking themselves against the walls and ceilings. The perfect insect feeds upon the foliage of trees, and is more or less destructive. The eggs are deposited in the earth, and hatch in about a month. The grubs remain in the ground, doing little injury till the second summer, when they attack the roots of plants. They remain as grubs in the earth for nearly three years, by which time they reach a length of two inches, and often appear in such great numbers as to do immense damage. The body of the grub is soft and of a dirty white, and its head is of red and brown, and its habit, like the cut worm, is to coil into a ball when disturbed. Like other grubs, they are difficult to poison, the best plan being to endeavor to destroy the beetles in early spring. This worm is eaten by skunks, coons, moles and birds. Dogs can be trained to eat it, and when so trained will follow a plow all day long.

Wire Worm.—The wire worm is a long, yellow, slender-bodied grub, with exceedingly hard and tough skin. These worms destroy the seed and young plants of squash, pumpkin, melon, and often potatoes. They are the grubs of snap-beetles, brown-black insects which, when laid over on their backs, have the singular power of snapping and springing violently to their feet. The writer has frequently seen grains of corn a week after planting, bored out to a shell, and containing as many as a dozen worms ravenously finishing the remainder of the grain.

Cut Worm.—Cut worms are the larvæ of various species of night moths which deposit their eggs late in the summer. When hatched, the worms enter the ground and remain in a torpid state all winter. In the spring they appear as naked, greasy, smooth caterpillars, ravenously attacking the seed, roots and stems of almost any young vegetable, and when disturbed, coiling quickly into a ball. The best method of killing them is to catch them by digging. They are sometimes destroyed by Paris green sprinkled on small bunches of freshly cut grass laid upon the surface of the soil where the worms are known to be. White hellebore has been found effective in the destruction of this pest.

Colorado Potato Beetle.—The Colorado potato beetle is, perhaps, one of the best recognized of insect pests, being large in size, and found in every locality. Its favorite foods are the leaves of the potato, tomato and egg plant. But it is readily destroyed with Paris green.

Squash Beetle.—The striped squash beetle, preying upon cucumbers and melons, is an insect a little over a quarter of an inch long, with a black and yellow jacket bearing three parallel black bands. The full grown beetle appears in the middle of spring, just in time to catch the plants as they sprout, eating the young leaves as they develop, so that the gardener almost gives up in despair of ever securing plants with too well developed leaves, at which stage they are usually considered proof against the beetles; but this is not always the case, for in some seasons plants of squash, cucumber, melons, pumpkin, having six or seven leaves large as a man's hand, are completely eaten off in a single day. Applications of Paris green, land plaster, slaked lime, must all be so applied as to reach the under side of the leaf as well as the top.

In gardens an effective way to keep off the mature flying beetles is to cover the seed hills at once, after planting, with square or circular frames, covered with mosquito netting, that the young plants may be protected from the beetles. The gardener may conclude he has conquered, but not so always, for the eggs of the same beetle, deposited in the earth, now hatched by the heat of the sun, develop larvæ, a little white worm, which, commencing at the vines under ground, pierce the stems through and through, to their utter destruction, and to the gardener's dismay. We recommend Hammond's slug shot to destroy the first brood of beetles which appears. This done, no larvæ will follow.

On Reedland Farm the Landreths, cultivating large breadths of watermelons and canteloupes, always have to replant, more or less, on account of the ravages of this troublesome insect, sometimes replanting five or six times, using an aggregate of nine or ten pounds of the seed to the acre before obtaining a complete growth, a very expensive process, increased cost of labor, of seed, and the risk of a delayed crop. On large areas the best remedy against this pest is slug shot, or Paris green, mixed with forty parts of land plaster or flour, and applied as often as it is washed off. Experiments made at Bloomsdale Farm have conclusively shown that various vine plants have different degrees of resistance to the noxious effects of Paris green, squashes being the strongest, pumpkins next, then cucumber, water melons and canteloupes least of all.

As the French wine growers kill the phylloxera insect feeding on the roots of the grape by the poisonous fumes of carbon bi-sulphide injected into the earth, why should not this same application destroy the white grub, wire and cut worm, squash beetle, and others? A spoonful of the liquid, injected by a syringe about the roots of the plants to be protected, might work wonders.

The Harlequin Cabbage Bug.—The harlequin cabbage bug is a very demon among garden pests, the perfect insect one-half inch long, somewhat resembling in shape a terrapin, having a hard shell brilliantly spotted. It is a sap sucker, puncturing the stalks and leaves of cabbage and other plants of the cabbage family, sucking out the sap and poisoning the entire plant. Turkeys and chickens decline to eat them, poison will not kill them, as they do not eat solid matter; they must be picked off by hand. This Mexican insect has repeatedly presented itself to the observation of the writer in such innumerable numbers as to obtain for itself a record of first place among destructive bugs. It is particularly fond of cabbage and turnip, attacking both in autumn and spring, and is especially destructive on those plants when shooting to seed. His firm has lost, on several occasions, sixty to seventy acres of cabbage, and still more of ruta bagas, even after weeks of labor and efforts to remove the bugs by hand picking; all being insufficient to check their numbers, and no poisonous application being effectual in checking their voracity. The most reliable method of meeting the ravages of this bug is to destroy the first brood at any cost, even of the crop itself.

Cabbage Worm.—The cabbage worm is a green caterpillar, feeding on nearly all broad-leaved vegetables, especially cabbage, cauliflower and lettuce. It is the larvæ of a white butterfly of European origin; Paris green will poison these caterpillars, but, except in the very early stages of cabbage growth, it is unsafe to apply so poisonous an article to a plant which might enfold the poisonous compound within its leaves and kill those who afterwards ate the plant. Pyrethrum has been found excellent as a destroyer, but probably Hammond's slug shot is as effective. Sometimes good results follow the application of white hellebore mixed with land plaster, four parts to one. In other cases a solution of one quart of powdered alum to twelve quarts of boiling water is effective. Sometimes good effects result from an application of a tablespoonful of pyrethrum mixed in two gallons of water, and applied forcibly with a spray syringe. The writer's experience with the cabbage worm dates from the period of its southern raid from Canada, where it was first established as an emigrant from Europe. He has had annoyance from it in variable degrees every year, but never to that serious extent as reported from localities where it has occasionally destroyed entire crops of cabbage.

Cabbage Louse.—The Downy cabbage louse is a mealy, soft-bodied insect, sometimes appearing in thousands, swarming like bees upon the leaves of young cabbage, Brussels sprouts and cauliflower. It can be driven off by application of Hammond's slug shot. Personal experience should always enable one to express opinions on a subject, and the writer, having had years of combat with this plant louse, looks upon it as a pest to be dreaded, difficult to kill, and destructive in its work. He has seen, upon the seed farm of his firm, as much as one hundred and fifty acres of otherwise healthy turnip plants, and one hundred acres of cabbage in the seed producing condition, entirely destroyed within three weeks. It is especially fond of the tender seed stems of the ruta baga, and in nearly all seed-growing districts where ruta baga seed-growing has been pursued twenty years, the cultivation has ceased entirely on account of the great increase of this insect. On young turnips the louse can be destroyed by dusting with Paris green, hellebore and slug shot, but as the insect enters the most intricate folds of the leaves of cabbage, cauliflower and Brussels sprouts, the poisonous applications cannot be used. An effective remedy, on small garden plots, is kerosene emulsion, made as follows: One part sour milk, two parts kerosene, thoroughly mixed by rapid agitation till the combination forms a creamy liquid. To this add fourteen parts water, and apply by an injector, or dash over the vines with a broom; or the emulsion may be made with: One quart soft soap, one quart kerosene, two quarts water mixed by forcible agitation, and diluted with sixteen quarts of water applied forcibly with a syringe.

Onion Fly.—The grub of this insect attacks the bulbs of onions, the tops of which grow yellow and soon die. There is no stopping its ravages, but prompt action should be taken to destroy the larvæ, as a preventive against a like attack the succeeding year. All sickly onions should be removed and burned, and from four to eight bushels of salt applied to the acre.

Turnip Fly.—The turnip fly, or flea beetle, is a jumping insect about one-twentieth of an inch in diameter, feeding on lettuce, radish, turnip and cabbage, as soon as they break through the ground, often destroying an entire crop, acres in extent, before the planter knows the seed has sprouted. Equal parts of wood ashes and land plaster dusted very thoroughly on the young plants will generally drive them off. An application of some efficiency is, one part of Paris green, mixed with forty or fifty parts of land plaster or flour. Some of the State legislatures have very admirably passed laws making it obligatory on farmers to destroy the Canada thistle, and other weeds dangerous to the interests of agriculture. No less caution should be observed with respect to certain insects, as, for instance, the potato beetle, multiplying by hundreds of thousands on the land of a slovenly farmer, infests the entire district next year, no matter how diligently other farmers apply themselves to its eradication.

Insects attacking garden plants may, in a slight degree, compensate for their injuries, by the agreeable study they afford to one of an investigating turn of mind. The eggs can be gathered and hatched under glass, or, better, under wire gauze, and the larvæ of many species observed passing through the various transformations to the fully developed winged insect. Flying insects can be caught in a scoop net placed on the end of a pole, and, when caught, can be killed by suffocation by the fumes of ammonia, or, more promptly, by chloroform or ether. Beetles can be killed by fumes of cyanide of potassium in a corked bottle, but this is recommended cautiously, as its fumes are a deadly poison.

CHAPTER XI.

Diseases of Garden Vegetables.

However much insect depredations may be dreaded by the gardener, he, at least, has some recourse against the grubs, worms, snails, caterpillars and bugs, by destroying them after some trouble, or by holding them in check by poisonous applications, so as finally to secure a crop. Not so, however, with fungous growths, which, intimately connected with the structure and circulation of the host plant, cannot always be destroyed by solutions poisonous to vegetable growth, for, with the fungus, the supporting plant may suffer equally with the parasite.

The Legislature of the State of New York has set a good example by the passage of a law authorizing the officers of the State Agricultural Society to enter upon farm lands of citizens of that State, where new or dangerous parasitic plants are found upon vines, or other plants, and to destroy the crops by fire, the State assuming the loss to the farmers.

The reader of this little volume may conclude that the author has adopted a singular method of promoting amateur gardening, by presenting to the beginner all the evils which can possibly occur to crush the ardor and forestall the labors of the young gardener. Not satisfied with dwelling on insect pests infesting gardens, he must here present a dissertation on diseases.

The observing man already knows that all vegetable life, like the animal, is subject to disease and decay. He has seen strong forest trees with lifeless branches, and fruit trees, as the peach and pear, cease to be productive. Garden vegetables of weaker development cannot be expected to be exempt, and a very brief survey of the prevalent diseases of a few varieties of field and garden plants may be instructive, and lead to such subsequent critical observation as may be of profit; as, for many of the diseases of vegetables, there are treatments which may be termed preventive, palliative or curative, and their proper use may, in time, reduce what is now a serious loss in garden products.

Many of the diseases are the result of unclean soil, which, like an unclean house, is a hotbed of infection; some are of a foreign origin, brought to this country with seeds and plants, and, as in the case of certain people, flourishing with double vigor under new conditions of life. Other diseases, again, of American origin, are carried, like certain insects, from one region to another by our transportation lines; as, for instance, the Colorado potato beetle, which has flourished for hundreds of years in Colorado and on the plains of Arizona, and southward into Mexico, but it never escaped from its natural habitat till our cultivated frontier reached its home, and then it spread East and North by easy stages on the potato fields.

Potato-Vine Fungus.—The potato is subject to the attacks of several parasitic fungi, two or more of which attack clover and lettuce, appearing as patches of white film, which, in a few weeks, spread over the entire plant, extract the juice and reduce the vigor of the plant so that growth of tubers ceases. There is no remedy for this disease, and to prevent its spread exceedingly great caution has to be observed in burning all the stems of the infected crop. To dress the land with lime and to cease to raise potatoes on the same ground for two years is the best system to pursue. A second fungus growth to which the potato is subject also attacks tomato and egg plants, on each of which it is equally injurious. It appears about midsummer, and flourishes most vigorously during close humid weather. It is first seen as a fine white bloom, accompanied by darker spots on the leaves. It is to be found mainly beneath the leaves, and if the temperature continues moist it rapidly distributes itself over the entire plant, the darker spots, increasing in number and size, indicating the presence of mycelium within the tissues soon ready to develop a white material on the surface. An offensive odor is an accompaniment of this disease. The fungus, under conditions favorable to its growth, develops rapidly, sometimes appearing and destroying a crop in two days, but always the germs of disease have been present beforehand, possibly for weeks. The stems of the entire crop should be burned, the land should be limed, and any succeeding crop planted with seed from a district not infected with the fungus, and the crop planted wide apart between rows to admit of a thorough circulation of air.

Cabbage Fungus.—Club-root in cabbage is a name applied to the outward results which appear on cabbage, turnips, mangels, carrots, as a distortion and enlargement, in spindle form, of the main root stem and rootlets, occasionally to ten times the normal size of the roots. This ugly growth is due to the attack of a fungus which usually fastens itself upon the plant at an early stage, and when once present remains permanently. The spores seem to form a connecting link between the vegetable and the animal kingdom, for though entirely vegetable, they have tail-like appendages which, by vibration, cause the spores to move over wet surfaces in quite a life-like manner. Cabbage with club-root—and no one can mistake the disease—should at once be burned, and no attempt made upon that land to grow cabbage for at least a year.

Pea Fungus.—A fungus attacking peas, especially late varieties, or early ones sown late, and known as pea mildew, is developed by decaying material of weeds or rubbish, and is forwarded, especially, under conditions of moisture and heat. When a crop is once attacked there is little hope of arresting its ravages, and the best course is to pull up the plants and use the ground for something else.

The Bordeaux Mixture, used to destroy fungus growths, as scab and mildew on grapes, apples, pears, and other fruits of hard wooded plants, is valuable also in the treatment of garden vegetables and flowers suffering from fungus. To make the mixture, take four pounds fresh unslaked lime, six pounds copper sulphate powdered, forty-five gallons of water, or in same proportion; slack the lime, making a creamy mixture. Pour into a barrel, straining it through a sack. Fill up with water and stir. The mixture will cost about one cent per gallon.

The mixture must be applied in the form of fine spray, applied with force by an effective pump or syringe. For fruits it will be safe to make four sprayings.

1st. Just as the flowers are opening. 2d. Ten days later, and so on at intervals of ten days. Sometimes six or seven sprayings are beneficial.

CHAPTER XII.

Heredity in Plants.

Breeders of horses, horned cattle, sheep and swine, acknowledge that merit or demerit is inherited, and it is the same with plants; they can be improved by selection and cross breeding, as the sexes are almost as distinctly developed in vegetables and flowers as in animals, and, with a few exceptions, present themselves to our notice in three forms, viz. :

Sexes in Plants.—First—Bi-sexual, in which both sexes are present as part of the flower, as seen in the fully developed pistil and stamens of the apple and pear, the cabbage and radish.

Second—Monœcious, in which the sexes are found in distinct flowers produced by the same plant, as in corn, melon, cucumber, squash.

Third—Diœcious, in which the sexes are borne on distinct plants, as asparagus and spinach.

Remote Parents of Cultivated Varieties.—The cabbage grower of to-day would scarcely recognize, in the coarse wild cabbage of the seashore of Denmark, the parent of our improved varieties; nor the celery lover the bitter plant, as found in its native habitats; nor the epicure in watermelons the bitter, indigenous melons found covering whole districts in Africa. The present development in plants is the result of heredity in selected specimens. The original individuals of every garden vegetable and every garden flower were caught, tamed and improved through cultivation and selection, covering longer or shorter periods of time. The same work of selection and improvement of good qualities in vegetables is yet going on, and more earnestly than ever before. The seed grower of to-day is doing the work, the only fear is he is going too fast, introducing many variations of little merit, rather than devoting himself to the selection and preparation of varieties of suitable quality.

Selection of Varieties.—Were it not for heredity the seed growers' labors would be in vain, but, fortunately, the man who finds a good thing in the greenhouse, flower garden, vegetable garden, or in the field, can seize upon it, and, by the aid of heredity, fix, after a time, its valuable qualities for the benefit of all. But it may be well to say he meets with many instances of curious reversion to original types.

Change of Seed.—It is quite possible to grow the same crop on the same land for successive years, but it is a ruinous policy. We own a plantation in Virginia, upon a field of which, it is said, corn was grown successively and uninterruptedly for ninety years, but the product had fallen to ten bushels per acre. The avoidance of such a course of seeding is known as the system of rotation of crops, that is, such an alternation of seeding as to complete define a cycle of cropping in a term of years. Now, no less important is a rotation in the seed itself. The vegetable gardener generally purchases his seeds from various sources, but the grain farmer sometimes blindly adheres to his own stock of wheat, rye, oats, till it has lost its original character, and run down in productiveness for want of healthy stamina.

Much is gained, then, by a change of seed of any family of plants, by seed grown on a different soil; and we urge our readers to make trial every year of a limited quantity, be it only a few papers, or pounds, of old or new varieties from localities different from their own in soil and climatic conditions. Many fungus growths in cultivated plants are superinduced by a weak physical development, so that everything points to the advantage of a change of stock if a cultivator wants to make either a reputation in the community for good crops or a profit on his product.

The gardener cannot change the climate of a locality, but he can transport plants from one end of the earth to the other and, subjecting them to new conditions of climate and soil, thus bringing about a variability which, by selection and continued culture, can be perpetuated, the new quality becoming hereditary. This process of selection has given us our best types of vegetables and flowers.

Man can do little to cause variability, but he can seize upon good forms when they do appear, and, by annual selection in fixed lines, secure important results. No doubt the edible plants of the older forms have been handed down from days of barbarism, when man was forced, at times, by hunger to eat almost anything he could swallow, but their qualities have been improved.

At this day we can hardly believe that the wild species of carrot, parsnip and cabbage were the progenitors of our cultivated varieties. Several years ago the wild carrot of the fields was experimented with at Bloomsdale Farm, and, after seven years of high culture and careful selection, it had developed a root quite soft, juicy and palatable. The writer has grown quite good-sized and fairly edible tubers, after five years of cultivation, from the wild potato of Mexico.

The work of selection and the results of heredity is in no plant so clearly shown as in the cabbage, every one of the two hundred, or more, forms being developed from one original,—the wild plant of the sea coast of western Europe, now developed into plants of many different characters, as kale, when the terminal and lateral leaf buds are active and open; as Brussels sprouts, when each leaf bud forms a head; as cabbage, when the terminal leaf bud alone is active, forming one head; as cauliflower, when the terminal flower bud is checked, producing a mass of succulent, edible, and, to a large extent, abortive flowers.

The occasional appearance of the so-called pod corn, otherwise primitive corn, developing among cultivated species, may be the result of heredity, as it is quite possible the original maize was of this character, every grain being covered by a distinct husk. But it is in the "melon family" that the greatest variations occur; possibly there are four thousand varieties known, comprising great variability in size, form and color of vine, and color, shape and size of fruit and form of seed, one variety being two thousand times larger than another. Nearly all of this family will interbreed; the canteloupe and cucumber have been hybridized on Bloomsdale Farm and grown there for several years as an interest-freak of nature.

While heredity is a well marked principle in vegetable life, there is a constant tendency to depart from established forms, sometimes for the better, oftener for the worse, for reversion is generally downward in the scale of excellence. The reversion may be in the form of a wild sport, or a distinct reproduction from a late or a very remote ancestor.

Every experienced seed grower knows that the purest crops will sometimes develop the wildest sports, for instance, a crop of cabbage of apparently absolute purity may produce a few plants like collards, the result alone of reversion. The seed grower is powerless to prevent this natural physiological freak, and the gardener who knows anything of seed production and vegetable variability deals more rationally with the seedsman than he who knows nothing of such matters, but thinks nature should produce plants all as much alike as nickels from the mint.

CHAPTER XIII.

Saving Seed.

Gardening at the present day is quite distinct from that of the past, for, while it has been, from ancient times, termed an art, it may now, in its advanced condition, be termed an art supported, explained and dignified by nearly every science, all being called upon to account for the natural phenomena of plant germination, vegetation and maturity.

Though very few market gardeners are scientific men, still, the progressive one nowadays gives considerable thought to matters truly scientific. For instance, the chemical results affecting plant development through the application of salts, of potash, soda, and other chemical substances used as fertilizers, upon soils of sedimentary, drift, or alluvial formation. For example, green sand marly soils, requiring distinct applications from soils of decayed red sandstone, and again, scientific, as respects botanical and physiological differences, plant subsistence, pollination, reversion, etc.

Systematic results, as affects species, can now generally be accounted for by the thoroughly intelligent student of plant life and culture, and if system is pretty well assured and the causes of such results fairly understood, gardening is on the direct road to become a science, and is certain to be so classed by the end of the century, though of course, in its higher walks, having but few practitioners amid the nations of the earth.

Few farmers or gardeners have the patience, the inclination or the training, to be close observers of the habits of plants under different climates and soils, frequently so modified as to appear in new forms, the modifications covering all the results of pollination and selection; consequently those who have acquired this habit of observation are marked men in their respective communities.

The variations in cultivated plants, due to the fancy or caprice of the seed grower, is not the only difficulty experienced by the purchaser of seeds who desires particular qualities; but equally difficult is the identification of fruits, flowers and vegetables under the various names by which they are sold, some particular varieties having a dozen names in as many locations, indeed, as many in the same locality. Of course, this can only be corrected by the natural determination among seed growers and seed merchants to refrain from the manufacture of names to advance the sale of their stocks in hand, but this is not likely to be soon realized, as there is no court or authoritative bodies to forbid the multiplication of names. Nevertheless, an effort is now being made to have established by Congress a national plant register, which, it is designed, shall give the description and history of every newly introduced fruit, vegetable, grain, flower or fiber, the record being official and authoritative. The bill, however, if passed, will not prevent Tom, Dick or Harry from introducing a plant by whatever name, good or bad, old or new, and the utmost that can be expected is that honest originators will register their introductions, and even some of these may not, through studied purpose or caprice.

In England an official record has been kept for years by the Royal Horticultural Society, which issues certificates to the exhibitors, for the first time, of new plants of merit. The introducers of good plants thus get a society notice, which is generally copied in all the agricultural or horticultural journals, but the plant is very likely to appear the next year under a half dozen new names, though of course it can never again be registered. However, this renaming does not prevent it from being sold at very high prices, for the more extravagant the name and the higher the price the more dupes to buy it. Every gardener can save seed by permitting certain of his plants to stand long enough, but usually such a course does not pay, for the reason that garden space is generally so valuable that crops reaching edible condition must be cleared away to make room for others in their season, and again, that on fields of limited extent, crops of various sorts of peas, beans, corn, melons, squash and cucumber become each within its own family hybridized, or interbred, so that crops grown from seed raised in the garden present in one lot all the qualities of the various crops of the preceding year, and always the poor qualities will be found to predominate, as with vegetable, like animal life, the coarse, ill bred types are the most precocious and prolific. Still, it is occasionally worth the time and labor of the amateur to experiment in seed saving, for it certainly affords interesting instruction, whether the return be profitable or not, and it cannot be doubted that the very cross-fertilizing, consequent upon the crowding of crops in gardens, has been the origin of many valuable hybrids. This cross-fertilizing occurs during the flowering season, and results from the pollen, a light powder, produced by the organs of the male flower of one sort of bean, corn, melon, or other plant, falling upon the female organ of the flower of some other variety of the same family. The pollen, carried by the wind, or borne on the bodies of insects, may be carried for miles. Corn has been known to intermix when planted hundreds of yards apart, or on opposite sides of a dense woodland, or on opposite sides of a river a mile in width. This natural disposition of established sorts to cross-breed has been taken advantage of by expert gardeners desiring to unite in one individual the good qualities of others. For instance, a very early pointed cabbage may be crossed with a very late flat one. with the view of producing a variety, uniting the good qualities of both; or with canteloupes, a poor variety with a showy netting may advantageously be crossed with a rich flavored sort without netting, and the result be a very desirable development, and so on with other plants without limitation.

The gardener, possessing a greenhouse, can conduct experiments in hybridizing with more convenience and certainty in results than in the open garden, as inclement weather will not interfere with his labors, nor insects defeat his purposes by crossing his selected plants from unknown sources.

Seed Growers.—The professional seed grower aims to produce his general stock of seed without hybridization. He starts with approved forms and, growing them apart, endeavors to strengthen or extend the desirable qualities of size, color, flavor, hardiness, or time of maturity. But all seed growers do not look upon a vegetable or fruit with the same eye and mind, consequently their conceptions of merit vary, and so do the plants which they pick out for select stock for the ensuing year. Thus it comes that seeds sold under the same name produce very different types of plants. One sugar corn grower may select his Evergreen, with short jointed stocks, having ears near the ground; another may pay no attention to the position of the ears, but select his seed alone for the size and shape of ear and depth and lightness of grain; or one squash grower may, for years, choose his from which to save seed as respects closeness of setting upon the vine, outward shape and color of fruit; while another may dwell principally upon thickness of flesh texture and flavor. With this variability in the whims of seed growers, it cannot be wondered at that seeds sold under the same name produce widely different results as to development.

CHAPTER XIV.

Seedsmen's Novelties and Responsibilities.

There cannot be any good reason advanced why the seed grower should not seize upon and perpetuate vegetable hybrids or sports whenever they present new and desirable features, even though the plant, on the whole, is no better than some other well known sort. Novelties may often show no practical improvement, in any sense, being simply a variability of questionable utility in form, size or color; nevertheless, the effort to develop novelties has resulted in an improvement in vegetables and flowers to such an extent that, in the manner of general excellence, the cultivated plants of the present day are far in advance of those of twenty years ago.

Demand for Novelties.—Novelties in vegetables and flowers are all right, so far as they are true novelties, and selected by practical seed-growers, but, unfortunately, many so-called novelties are not the result of culture or selection by practical workers in the field, but altogether the product of the sensational seed merchant, who does his farming at his desk, his plow being his pen, drawn by an imagination so fertile as to have exhausted the vocabulary of the English language, to which he adds pictures and illustrations, ofttimes portrayed in such an undignified and offensive manner as to bring his business down to the level of the mountebank. In no business of the present day is there so much disguised humbug and open misrepresentation as in the seed business,—misrepresentation in description of color, form and merit of vegetables and flowers, due, on one hand, to ignorance, and on the other, to design, by illustration or pictures of monstrous and impossible vegetables and flowers; also in the illustration of seed stores, offices, seed-packing rooms, and published statements of sales, all schemes to catch the eye and take the money of the confiding gardener.

This reprehensible practice, originated by English seedsmen, has been adopted in this country, and, as Americans do not like to be outdone by Britons, they have gone, not one better, but advanced by strides and jumps, till the Englishman hides his head in abashment at his own insignificance.

It will, however, remain for the planter of novelties and specialties to determine for himself, whether they develop features of superior excellence upon his soil and under the conditions of his climate. On some soils they may possess very desirable qualities, and entirely fail on others. Merit in vegetables covers a wide range of character. It may consist of coloring, form, size, texture, flavor, precocity, productiveness, or freedom from disease, sunburn or decay, resistance to insect depredations, and excessive heat or cold, wet or drought. All these qualities are subjects for study in the field by the observing seed grower, market or private gardener, for these cannot be determined at the desk of the modern catalogue manufacturer. So much humbug has been thrown into the seed catalogues of the past ten years, that the intelligent gardener has had his eyes opened, and he is now discriminating between those dealers who can advise technically and those who have no training in the field.

Seedsmen's Responsibilities.

A review of the seed catalogues, price lists and publications of American, English, French and German seed merchants and seed farmers, will reveal the fact that they all disclaim responsibility for the consequences of planting seed obtained from them. They emphatically declare they cannot, and will not, be held responsible for the varying results of seed sold by them and planted by their customers, consequent upon influences of soil, rainfall, drouth, periods of sowing, inexperience of sower, and the many other causes which produce conflicting results in the germination of seed, development of plants, and in the perfection of growth, fruit or flower.

To clearly convey the position taken by European seed merchants upon this subject of responsibility, four forms of disclaimer, as published by as many well-known foreign seedsmen, are here given, all others using the same or similar forms:

1st. "We herewith desire to remind our customers, that whilst using our utmost care to supply seed only of such quality as to insure entire satisfaction, we give no warranty as to description, quality or productiveness, there being too many causes, known and unknown, which prevent good seeds from germinating."

2d. "We wish it to be distinctly understood, that while we exercise the greatest care to supply all seeds pure and reliable, we are not, in any respect, liable or responsible for the seeds sold by us, or for any loss or damage arising from any failure thereof."

3d. "We send out only seeds that will, to the best of our belief, give entire satisfaction; it must, however, be expressly understood that immunity from error being unattainable, and success more often dependent on climatic or local influences than is generally supposed, we warrant neither description, growth nor productiveness of any goods we sell, nor will we hold ourselves in any way responsible for the crop."

4th. "We give no warranty, express or implied, as to description, quality, productiveness, or any other matter of any seeds we send out, and we will not be, in any way, responsible for the crop. If the purchaser does not accept the goods on these terms they are at once to be returned."

No seedsman with any security to his property rights could conduct a business where he would be subject to suits at law by every merchant and gardener who might be inclined to lodge at his door the material results of crops. Every observing worker in the garden can recall most contradictory experience in the sprouting and growing of crops. For instance, in April, 1890, the writer drilled, on Bloomsdale Farm, many acres of bush beans of various sorts, and in the trial grounds planted samples of these and many other lots. These field crops and the trial ground plantings were repeated in May. The spring temperature was cold and the earth kept constantly cold and damp by frequent rains; the results were so contradictory as to be beyond explanation. For example, a special variety, doing well in the field, did badly in the trial ground; or the same variety, doing well in trial grounds, did badly in the field. In every case the highest results were accepted as indicative of the percentage of vitality, though the same lot of beans may have exhibited the wide range of from twenty-five to ninety-five per cent of germination.

The same irregular results are observable, not only in germination, but in subsequent growth, and all the way to maturity of form, size and quality of vegetable, fruit or flower from seed out of the same bag, all consequent upon natural or artificial condition of soil, temporary influence of temperature by day, and quite as often by night; sunlight, rainfall, favorable influence to urge into rapid growth, or unfavorable conditions to check progress often occurring at that period of the plant's development, determining its merit for excellence, mediocrity or inferiority.

Irregularity in sprouting is often observable with seeds just harvested, particularly so with corn and beans, as it would seem nature intended they should become dry or dormant before sprouting into new life. Seeds of cabbage, turnip and radish are liable to grow moldy if kept in bags without ventilation, and often the seed merchant is blamed for the inattention of the consumer himself.

The writer has known of many instances where freshly harvested, and, consequently, soft seeds of turnip, cabbage and radish, shipped because the consumer insisted upon having fresh seeds, proved, upon examination later on in the season, after having been kept in bags as shipped, to have taken on a moldy smell and, on trial, to have fallen from ninety or ninety-five per cent. vitality to fifty per cent. Sugar corn is very liable to injury when stored in bags, and new beans shipped early in autumn are almost certain to sweat.

In the United States the leading seedsmen publish a disclaimer to the same effect as their brethren in Europe, the phraseology, in general, being about the same. No sensible gardener would take exceptions to this, as it is only such a precaution as he himself would take, knowing full well the variable results of climate, soil, rainfall, and variations in the action of manures.

CHAPTER XV.

WEEDS.

An old adage among the English wheat growers is, "that the greatest weed in wheat is wheat," implying that a plant of wheat properly developed must have room, that crowding by another, even of its own species, is injurious, and that a plant so crowding another is a weed. A weed, then, is a plant out of place, not necessarily a noxious plant, or a wild plant.

The ordinary understanding adopts the term weed to designate an unattractive plant, without special value. On the farm the term weed is used to designate an intruder among cultivated crops, an uninvited guest. As a rule, those plants recognized as weeds are of foreign origin, the seed being brought to this country through commerce, transported here with other seeds, or in packing material of hay or straw. As an example may be cited the one hundred new plants which appeared and were scattered all over Fairmount Park after the Centennial Exhibition, which were mainly from the forty countries represented. The delicate ones succumbed under our cold winter; many of the hardy ones still exist, spreading far and wide over the surrounding country.

It is a curious fact to note that foreign weeds have taken a firmer place in our own garden and field than our aboriginal weeds, which have disappeared before the march of the invader as native tribes have succumbed before the descendants of the Europeans. All of our cultivated plants have their wild originals, and many of our most ornamental flowers have been discovered away from the haunts of man, but whatever the form, color or habit of plants, injurious to other crops or exhausting the soil without profit, they are designated as weeds.

Classification of Weeds.—These pestiferous plants may be divided into three classes: Annuals, developing seed and dying the same season; biennials, taking two years to perfectly develop and produce seed, and then die; perennials, covering several seasons of growth and seeding. These three classes may be divided as respects the character of underground growth, some producing surface roots, as rag weed, easily pulled up, others producing rod-shaped roots, as wild carrot, which can be extracted entire; other bulbs, as buttercups or garlic, very difficult of eradication, while others are tubers, as coco grass, a troublesome class, and still others, producing subterranean root-stems, as Canada thistle, having numerous buds, each capable of developing new plants.

Destroying Weeds.—All these weeds, when in their first stages of growth, may be kept in check, if not entirely destroyed, in the garden, by plucking them when an inch or so high, or with a hoe or knife cutting them off, or by disturbing the soil with a cultivator, by turning under with a plow, or by smothering with mulch or waste material. Noxious weeds never should be permitted to mature their seeds; if not destroyed they should certainly be so cut down and kept cut down as to prevent seed development.

State Laws Respecting Weeds—In some States there are legislative enactments requiring the destruction of the Canada thistle, recognized everywhere as one of the most persistent and dangerous of encroaching weeds. It would be well if a similar statute was adopted by all the States, and applied to other weeds, as mustard, ox-eye daisy, wild carrot, which careless farmers allow to propagate on their lands, to their own disgrace and to the manifest injury of their neighbors. A very intelligent French agriculturist, once visiting the writer, after making a tour of the United States, said the American farm was the most slovenly he had ever looked upon; and it is quite true, for, as a rule, every farmer in this country has more land than he can properly attend to, and, at the best, but few have had that education in the economy of space which has been so intently studied in Europe.

CHAPTER XVI.

Hotbeds and Cold Frames.

The ordinary size of a convenient hotbed, may be ten feet, by six or seven feet wide, or it may be only of the dimensions of a common window sash, three feet by four feet, more or less. The shape has nothing to do with the definition, which may be to the effect that a hotbed is a box covered with glass, the whole placed upon a bed of soil resting on a bed of fermenting stable manure, the heat from which, rising in the form of vapor, warms and moistens the soil within the box, while, at the same time, the sun's rays, passing through the glass, are retained to warm and vivify the surface.

Seeds sown within such a box will germinate in less time than without such protection. As an illustration of the varying forms which hotbeds may take, the writer may say that he once saw an efficient hotbed full of vigorous vines of egg plant, made of a large oil or whisky barrel, with the head and bottom knocked out, and then let down half way into the earth and banked up all around with soil. In the bottom, six inches of stone were placed for drainage, and then eighteen inches of rich, unfermented horse manure, six inches of fine rich earth, rising to within ten inches of the top of the barrel, the open top covered with a discarded window sash. We do not recommend such a hotbed, but it is an example of the simplicity with which one can be made. With a full understanding of the cardinal principles of so applying the manure as to make it hold the heat of fermentation, to handle the sash so as to collect and accumulate the sun's heat, it matters little what form the box assumes.

The location of the hotbed has much to do with its success or failure. It should only be placed on land always free from flooding, preferably on a declivity, with good subsoil drainage, sheltered from cold winds, and facing south or southeast. As an example of a hotbed frame, we will describe it as a box for one, two or four sashes, each seven feet long by three and one-quarter feet wide. This dimension of sashes is given because it is easy to handle. The width named will allow for four lengths of 8x10 glass placed lengthwise. Whatever the dimensions of the sashes, all should be alike, so as to be interchangeable. The frame may be permanent, of brick or stone, or, temporary, of boards. The frame may be regularly built by a carpenter, with strong corner pieces, or the gardener can do all the work himself and attain just as practical results. Doing the work himself, he may proceed as follows: The length and breadth of the bed having been decided upon, excavate a space two feet wider and two feet longer than the indicated dimensions. After the excavation is completed, drive down at the four corners, and at intervals between the corners, posts of proper lengths, four by four inches square, to which nail the side boards; the posts on the back of the frame rising twelve to fifteen inches above the surface level, and those in front of the frame six to eight inches, nailing the boards only to those portions of the post which are above the earth level, the boxes, as it were, standing on stilts, it being desirable to use as little lumber as possible. The excavation is for the purpose of keeping the material and contents of the bed as much removed as possible from frigid air currents, and thus economize manure.

Into the excavations of eighteen or twenty inches in depth throw one foot in thickness of cornstalks, leaves, half rotten straw and coarse manure, these principally for preventing dampness or facilitating drainage; on top of this coarse strata spread a layer of three to four inches of good horse-stable manure just beginning to ferment, avoiding pig and cow manure, as they do not heat. The manure for hotbeds must be well manipulated, that the fermentation may be prolonged, and this is best done by shaking out the manure loosely with forks, and, if exceedingly rich, mixing it with some poorer material, otherwise the fermentation will be too fierce and of too short duration; indeed, to secure thorough mixing, it is well to turn the manure intended for hotbeds at least three times, at intervals of two days, and, when transferring the manure from the pile to the bed, it should be done quickly, that the manure be as little exposed to the chilling influence of the air as possible.

Tramp the manure down and spread it evenly from end to end and side to side; when done repeat with a layer of three or four inches, and when this is spread and well tramped down, add a third layer of the shortest and best unfermented manure, as this subsequently will be a feeding ground for plants, the various layers of manure making twelve to fourteen inches in total depth. If the spreading and tramping and quality of material be not regularly distributed in the bed, it will be irregular and the plants the same. For early beds use the manure liberally. Very late beds can be made without any, as the sun, in late spring, will give sufficient heat.

Manure for Hotbed.—As fresh horse-stable manure, when used alone, is very heating and soon subsides, it is best to mix it with leaves or half rotten straw, as seed may be burned over manure of too high temperature. Of course it is impossible to indicate fixed dates for sowing, over a country so broad as this, and with such a variety of climatic conditions. The beginner can get his best hints for procedure from a gardener resident in his district, or others not far removed from it. Any recommendations here simply apply to the Atlantic Middle states, and even there the practice is very diverse. Tomatoes and egg plants are best sown from the first to the fifteenth of March, otherwise they attain too large a size before a right opportunity for transplanting may present itself.

The writer, and all others of experience, find it always best to make two sowings. Cost of seed is a matter of little importance, as compared with securing a satisfactory stand of plants. A gardener had better pay three dollars per pound for good seed than one dollar for seed that will not germinate, or, still worse, to prove, after germinating, to be of inferior quality, as thus his time and labor would be wasted. As it is always desirable to have the crop started ahead of the weeds natural to the soil, the writer suggests the soaking of the seeds before the bed is made, that when the bed arrives at the proper condition the seed may have germinated and be ready to sow.

Sowing Seeds in Hotbeds.—With either tomato, egg plant or cabbage, mix the seed with three times its bulk of sifted sand, white sand preferred, that the seed may be better distributed; soak in tepid water for one hour and place the mixture of sand and seed in shallow boxes or pans, carefully labeled, and kept in a warm place till the seeds show signs of germinating. Some varieties will take longer than others, and different crops of the same variety will take different periods to sprout. Seed thus treated and sown on a properly prepared bed will often show a green line twenty-four hours after sowing, and thus be several days ahead of the weeds. If the bed is ready before the seed can be prepared, as described, then sow the dry seed and trust to sun, manure and water to hasten the process of germination. After sowing keep the surface moist. Seed started in pans may not need more than one watering previous to showing above ground. Dry seed may require three or four waterings, but the gardener must judge of this for himself, keeping the soil moist, but not wet, to the depth of one inch.

Care of Hotbeds.—Hotbeds should be covered early in the evening, to retain their heat, and in the morning uncovered when the sun rests upon the glass, as every effort should be made to give the plants all the sunlight possible, as its rays are vivifying to a degree beyond the amount of its heat, it having a chemical and physiological effect beyond explanation. Even dull light is better than no light, consequently it is a bad plan to cover sashes with mats, except for the direct purpose of keeping out cold.

If the box should be much charged with steam from the manure, let it off at the high side, otherwise the vapor may cause the plants to damp off. This damping off is a very serious matter, usually due to a want of ventilation, and it will occur whether there be steam or not in the box, unless the air be changed, as it really seems to become poisonous; consequently the bed should be aired, even in cloudy and cool weather. The amount of air should be regulated by the amount the crop will stand without injury. By such proper treatment the plants will be short, stocky, with broad, green leaves; with too little air the plants will be long-legged, yellow and sickly.

Do not endeavor to obtain, by the exclusion of the outside air, that heat which the manure and sun should supply. By close attention to watering, airing and early afternoon closing, the development of hotbed plants may be advanced ten days over others not so carefully looked after. It may be in place here to observe that much trouble may be saved by having all the sashes of uniform dimensions, as, if interchangeable, by a little good management a few sashes will often serve twice the number of boxes; for, by moving the sashes along as the sowing progresses, their places being supplied by board coverings, much can be accomplished.

After hotbed plants reach from two to three inches in height, they may be transplanted to other boxes or frames. These frames may be filled with good soil, heating manure being unnecessary, as the sun's rays in April or May should afford sufficient heat to advance them to a healthy growth. The soil in these frames should rest on a ten-inch drainage bed of rough manure, cornstalks, or trash, and should preferably be of two layers of distinct consistency, one a heavy soil on top of the drainage material, with three inches of light sandy soil on top of it. By this means the plants can be taken up for setting out in the open ground without injury to their fiber, which would be the case if the surface layer was of compact loam. The experienced gardener collects in the autumn the soil for his hotbeds, well knowing that Jack Frost, at the time he wants his hotbed soil, generally has it tightly locked up in an icy embrace.

Transplanting Tender Plants.—Do not transplant to the field too early. It is best to cut tomatoes back to two inches when four inches high, which operation makes them stocky, new buds will appear at each leaf stem, while the root will become more fibrous. Indeed, tomatoes well cut back and given plenty of air need not be transplanted from original beds, but can go directly into the garden. Eighty feet square of hotbed surface drilled in rows at five inches apart should produce enough plants to cover one acre of ground. Tomatoes grown in open air outside beds should plant one acre to each one hundred and fifty square feet. Seedlings grown in outside beds need not be transplanted before removal to a permanent position in the field. At Bloomsdale, plants set out May 10th to 20th ripen fruit by July 4th.

During the operation of transplanting, the newly planted bed should be shaded and watered as the work progresses, keeping the shade on for two days, removing it in the evenings or during rainy weather, after which the plants may have the full benefit of the sun's rays. In the evenings water sufficiently to keep the soil moist, and give plenty of air, while avoiding chilling them, and in a couple of weeks the plants will be ready to remove to the field. Egg plants take more heat than tomatoes, but they need as much ventilation and should have more room.

Cabbage, cauliflower and lettuce sow broadcast, first raking the surface soil to the finest tilth, distributing the seed so that about ten seeds will fall to the square inch; this many, to allow for unvital seeds, for too deep or too shallow covering, and for insect depredations. Rake as lightly as possible, so as not to cover more than one-eighth of an inch; water, using a watering pot with a very fine rose nozzle, or dash on water with a broom, and put on the sash.

Tomatoes, egg plants and peppers should be sown in rows, raking the surface soil to the finest tilth, and with a triangular stick of a length equal to the width of the box, press the sharp edge down into the fine soil, making straight parallel rows, or trenches, three inches apart, and not over one-half inch in depth. Drop the seeds in the row, five to eight seeds to the inch, of egg plant or pepper, and of tomatoes quite ten to the inch, cover over one-third inch deep with light soil from both sides of the trench, gently tapping the soil down with a shingle or light board, so as to bring the seed and earth into intimate contact. If the seed has been soaked and is mixed with wet sand, mix with some dry sand to make the mass friable. Sand will rather aid the germination than hinder it. When sowing germinated seed it must not be exposed to dry soil or wind, or it may be destroyed.

Stable manure hotbeds will, it may be presumed, continue to be used, in spite of the cheapened construction and completer development of beds and glass houses, heated by fire, cheap as they are, for they are too costly for some, take too much time to erect, and require early preparation.

Forcing beds for hot air heating may have much the same appearance as manure hotbeds, and may be cheaply made by excavating a pit, or trench, a foot deeper than described for the making of manure hotbeds, and laying in the pit a double line of iron or terra cotta smoke pipe leading from a furnace placed in a deeper pit at one end of the line to the extreme end of the excavation, and back to a chimney built alongside or on top of the furnace, that the heat from the furnace, warming the cold air in the chimney, may drive it out, and thus, creating a partial vacuum, start a steady current throughout the entire length of the hot air flues.

Nearly fifty years ago this arrangement was in use on Bloomsdale Farm, though some people think it is a new idea. The smoke pipes in the bottom of the trench are covered over by a floor of boards to support the earth, the floor at the end next to the furnace being twelve to fifteen inches above the pipes, but at the other end approaching to within six inches, because of the loss of heat at the extremity.

Intermediate Bed. — The term "intermediate bed" may be applied to beds or frames used in the autumn for the propagation of lettuce, parsley and other crops intended to mature during winter. In sash beds two crops can be grown, first lettuce, again lettuce, with radish between the rows. The boxes should be on a dry piece of land and well sheltered from fierce blasts of wintry air.

To make the frame, drive or set posts into the ground, projecting above the surface, twelve inches on the back and eight inches on the front, the distance between the front and back lines being three inches less than the length of the sashes, so as to admit of an overhanging at both ends, to cast off water. Board up the two lines and the two ends, and the skeleton is completed. Next put in cross pieces at proper distances for the sash to run on; these can be mortised in at both ends. Next dig out the interior of the frames to a depth of ten inches, preserving the good top soil, and fill in the excavation with drainage material of trash, dead leaves and vines, strawy manure, or even shavings, well pressed down. On top of the filling of the pit place four to five inches of good surface soil, and on top of that a couple of inches of soil still better if it can be had, if not, work in some fine compost and some sand, raising the surface to within eight or nine inches of the glass. In sowing intermediate beds, proceed the same as in sowing hotbeds. If old hotbeds are used the preparation for the seeding, consists in turning over the surface soil, and possibly adding two inches of fresh sandy compost.

Cold Frame.—A cold frame is a winter storage box containing plants to be transplanted into hotbeds, or in the field in spring. It is always made without manure, and may be made without underdrainage, though such drainage always has its advantages. If made for merely temporary use, the front and back boards may be held by stakes driven down on each side of the boards to hold them in place. The cross pieces used in hotbeds and intermediate beds are not needed in cold frames, which are intended to be kept in a dormant state; therefore no warmth is necessary, and no glass is needed except in extremely cold weather. Sometimes the plants are started in the frame in the early autumn, other times they are taken from other localities and dibbled in, or laid in or bedded very closely, the aim being to suspend or retard growth. Plants in cold frames, when frozen, must not be exposed to the sun, but on mild days plenty of air should be given to keep them sound and healthy.

Plant Pit.—A pit for plants is used for housing or protecting during winter half hardy plants, many of which, in a well constructed pit, blossom during winter and will all be well advanced in spring. In general principles a plant pit is similar to a cold frame bed, made more durable, and also set deeper in the earth.

To construct a cheap plant pit, select a dry location and mark off the length desired, and of width equal to the length of sashes used. As the contents of a cold pit are intended to stand from autumn to spring it, should be placed on land not likely to be flooded by rain, melting snow or back water. Plant pits may be for permanent or temporary use, and of either brick or wood. If of wood, a solid frame may be used, made by setting or driving posts in two parallel lines, the back line twenty inches higher than the front; or dig out the earth to a depth of two feet and set square sided posts at the corners, and along the sides to which nail on boards, making a box without a bottom or top within the excavation. The posts on the back should be three and one-half feet long. On top of the frame place six covered bars, at proper intervals, for the sash to slide upon the ends of the bars mortised into the back and front boards of the frame. Pack the earth tightly in the cracks beneath the surface around the outside of the box, and above the surface bank up all around with the excavated earth. The pit is now ready for the reception of potted plants of primulas, pelargoniums, violets, wall flowers, begonias, heliotropes, fuchsias, abutilons, lilies or roses, the tallest plant being placed on the back, where the elevation is three and one-half feet.

CHAPTER XVII.

Market Gardening Under Glass.

So many and so radical have been the changes in modern commercial gardening during the last twenty-five years that a practical market gardener, of a quarter of a century ago, who, like Rip Van Winkle, should have taken a sleep from 1870 until the present, on awaking would find that his profession, as he understood it, had passed away, his old-fashioned and pet methods having been so altered that he would neither recognize nor understand the ways and means in practice by his scientific successors. Similar improved methods and appliances run through every branch of horticulture, but there is no branch where there have been more innovations made than in that of forcing vegetables under glass. These various changes in modes of culture are the result of a rapidly increasing demand in large cities and towns in the north and west for lettuce, radishes, cucumbers and other esculents for winter and early spring use. To meet this constant, ever-broadening and profitable branch of gardening, new and improved systems had to be developed. As long as the art of gardening has been practiced, both for private advantage and, in a limited extent, for commercial purposes, forcing certain vegetables in winter has been customary, but the old methods, entailing a great amount of manual labor, were expensive, the cost, if taken into account, being often greater than the value of the articles produced. Every reading gardener knows that lettuce, asparagus, radish and cucumbers have, for a century, been grown during winter by bottom heat in glass covered hotbeds or in cold frames, which slow methods are in use yet by private gardeners for home consumption; but with the commercial market gardener, who aims for the largest net returns from his capital and labor, the old style hotbed and cold frame no longer answer the purpose, for they are expensive, as compared with returns, and do not enable him to meet the enormously increased demand for crisp winter-grown vegetables. In changing from the old to the present system, mistakes were made in the construction of the early forcing-houses, which time and practical experience have modified and corrected. Accordingly, such structures, built during the last eight or ten years, are very different in appearance and interior arrangements from those erected a dozen years ago. At that time the ordinary greenhouse form was imitated in constructing vegetable forcing houses. These were usually built eleven feet wide and as long as necessary, with side walls four feet high, the top roofed with movable sashes three by six feet. In such houses there were two tables three and one-half feet high running the whole length, with a narrow passage-way in the center. On these wooden tables, or benches, prepared soil, to a depth of twelve to fourteen inches, was placed, and made ready for the process of culture. The heating was done by hot water, the same as now. The water used was lifted by hand-worked force-pumps, and applied sometimes by hose, but generally by the expensive system of hand-pots, entailing a great amount of labor, a slow and expensive method compared with the system now practiced.

As stated, the form of houses and interior construction of those built recently are different in appearance and more economically arranged for the specific purpose of raising winter vegetables; the changes are but the results of practical experience in this branch of horticulture by some of the most thrifty and prosperous market gardeners in the vicinity of Philadelphia, where this system of market gardening is carried out on a most extensive scale. It may be of interest to briefly outline the construction of four distinct styles of forcing houses for vegetables, which may be designated as systems numbered 1st, 2d, 3d and 4th.

In reference to system No. 1 a progressive and successful market gardener in New Jersey has said: "I have built, in all, fourteen large vegetable forcing-houses, and the one that I have just completed I consider as near right as it is possible to get it, and that after an experience of twelve years in this branch of gardening." In this connection the fact may be mentioned, incidentally, that the gardener referred to is both thrifty and prosperous, the result of skill in conducting a business requiring a keen, practical and observing mind, with the energy and cash to carry out his plans. His is the kind of experience that is of real value to beginners, and my aim is to give, as concisely as possible, the substance of such experience, gathered from those who bought it dearly by hard work and disappointment in their first efforts. Facts, when gleaned from such sources, are of value to those who are about to embark in the same line of business. To be able to avoid the stumbling blocks and steer clear of the mistakes likely to be made in a new undertaking is of the utmost importance, as saving time and cash, two important considerations.

The forcing house recently constructed by the market gardener referred to and which may be designated as plan No. 1, is thirty-one feet wide, outside measure, two feet less inside, and two hundred and fifty feet long. The house is set down in an excavation, partly below the surface, the footwalks being thirty inches below the outside level. The exterior walls, four feet high, are built of brick, thirty inches below the surface and eighteen inches above it on the outside. The top of these walls is finished to receive a plate. The top of the house is a lean-to span with a hip-joint. The ridge-pole is eleven feet above the floor, and jointed. The pine strips running from the plate to the ridge-pole are one and one-half by two and one-half inches, made fast to a cross-piece at the hip-joint and ridge-pole, and are ten inches apart. Heavy French glass 8x10 is glazed on the outside of the strips. It is economy to use the best quality of glass for this purpose. Every twelve feet on both sides there is a hinged sash, running from the plate to the hip-joint. By this means the house can be aired when necessary, an operation of the utmost importance. With this exception the roof structure is made fast, avoiding the use of movable sashes entirely. The water, falling upon the roof, is all saved and led by gutters into a cistern at the end of the house, to be used for watering the plants when needed. As the rain falling upon the roof may not be sufficient, a well and pump are provided to meet cases of emergency. There are three tables, or beds, running the length of the house, and two narrow passage-ways. The center bed, which is eighteen feet wide, is made by erecting two parallel walls of brick, running through the length of the house to within six or eight feet of each end. These walls should be eight inches thick and three and one-half feet high. In digging the excavation for the house, the space designed for the center bed may be left intact, excepting the removal of the upper half. This block of natural soil is walled in, forming a solid bed distinct from the side beds, which are open beneath. Upon the bank of natural soil is placed well-rotted manure and garden soil preparatory to culture. Elevated beds (the exponents of this system claim), are more desirable than those sunken to the level of the floor, in the economy of heating, as well as in working, elevated ones being credited with producing more uniform crops than the others, at less expense. The use of brick instead of wood for the center table is an improvement in the method of construction which will strike every practical gardener favorably. In a house that is kept damp and warm several months of the year, wood will rot out every five years, and it is the experience of every gardener that the wooden tables have to be removed every five years, a very considerable item of expense in a large house. As a matter of fact, the first outlay, for brick and building the walls, is much more than wooden benches would cost, but the brick lasts as long as there is a roof kept over the house. Many instances may be cited where gardeners have been, and are now, making the change of substituting brick for wood on the basis of economy. As already stated, the side beds are not solid, as is the center bed, but are open for the location of hot and cold water pipes, it being very desirable, if not necessary, that these pipes be accessible at all points. The supports for these side tables, which are three and one-half feet wide, may be brick columns or wooden posts, with slate or boards for the sides and bottom. The same depth and quality of soil should be placed on the benches as on the center table. The roof of the forcing house is supported by three lines of iron rods, or pipes, one and one-half inches in diameter, and set about ten or twelve feet apart. One of these lines of support runs from the ridge-pole to the center of the middle bed, and the other two from the hip-joint to the edge of the side beds, thus holding the roof of the house. In the construction of vegetable-forcing houses the cost must naturally vary more or less in different localities on account of labor and material, the method of building and the finish put upon the houses. Estimates for the construction of such houses are within the reach of every gardener, including all the appurtenances to make the houses complete for use. Every horticultural journal gives, in its columns, the addresses of persons whose business it is to build houses of this description, and all other designs now in common use by practical, commercial gardeners. In the same journals can be found advertisements of all the leading manufacturers of heating apparatus.

The approximate cost of a vegetable forcing house, erected upon system No. 1, dimensions 30x250 feet complete, will not exceed $4,500. This comprises cost of boiler, hot and cold water pipes, about $1,700, and the pipes and cocks for watering about $100 more. Such a house may be heated by hot water carried in three lines of three-inch pipes running around under the side tables, or it may be heated by steam, the water being forced by natural circulation. This amount of heating surface is quite sufficient to keep the house at a temperature ranging from 40° to 50° during the most severe weather of mid-winter. In fact, all that is really necessary the coldest nights is to have heat enough to keep frost out of the house. In growing and forcing vegetables in winter there is nothing gained by having the temperature higher than here indicated. It is, on the contrary, detrimental to the healthy and vigorous growth of plants. In the latitude of Philadelphia it will take about fifteen tons of coal to heat a house of the size described during the cold months. The aim, in past days, to get a high temperature in forcing houses, was one of the serious and expensive mistakes made by gardeners when such structures were first substituted for hotbeds and cold frames. The want of success and, at times, the loss of all or a portion of the crop was, in the estimation of the more practical gardeners of the present day, often owing to overheating. A reduced amount of heat is less expensive, and, at the same time, the results are more satisfactory. In following the system of moderate heating there is less loss among soft-leaved vegetables from what gardeners term "damping off." This dreaded disease comes like a thief in the night, and works destruction with the crop. Instances are well known where one-half to two-thirds of a crop of lettuce, in large houses, has been destroyed by this "damping off" before the plants were half grown. It seems to be the fashion nowadays to attribute all obscure cases of mortality of plants under glass to "fungoid growth." A little science is a dangerous thing, and it would often be more practical to attribute it to a want of physical strength consequent upon unfavorable conditions.

The modern method of watering forcing houses is very different now from what it was formerly. In fact, the present system entails little labor; a half-grown boy, with good sense, can perform the work without difficulty. A pipe one and one-quarter inches in diameter connected with the steam pump and cistern, and then laid under the side benches with screw-tipped faucets arranged at intervals of twenty feet, so that a rubber hose may be attached, is the present form of apparatus. To the end of the rubber pipe should be fixed a rose, or sprinkler, twice or thrice as large as the rose on a large watering-pot; with this the watering can be done with ease and rapidity. The holes in the rose, or nozzle, should be small, so as to throw a large and fine spray of water over the beds. The frequency of watering depends altogether on the condition of the atmosphere. There are times when the beds should be watered daily, and, again, when once or twice a week will be quite sufficient. This is a matter that every practical gardener exercising common sense will soon settle in his own mind. The beds should be kept moist, without being soaked and soggy. As a matter of course, towards spring, when the sun is warm, the beds will need more moisture than in mid-winter, when the weather is cold and cloudy.

The estimate for labor for a house of the size described can only be approximately stated. Of course, there is nothing to be done inside of the house from June until October. Allowing a liberal compensation, the labor should not exceed three hundred dollars, and this may be considered an outside figure. With intelligent management and sufficient capital there is always sure to be a handsome profit realized on the investment.

Among the many successful market gardeners in the vicinity of Philadelphia, may be named Messrs. Mabbit & Wiles, Camden, N. J. This firm has a tract of six acres, nearly one-half of which is under glass, and so worked as to illustrate the profit which can be had by systematic management and practical experience. The style of construction of the houses of this firm may be designated as system No. 2.

The greater portion of these houses have surface beds, but some are fitted with elevated tables, these being the best for lettuce, cress and radish, which, grown in midwinter, require to be near the light, but, as cauliflower, a very important crop, a later and taller plant, does best on surface beds, much of the lettuce and cress has to be grown on the level.

These houses, built upon the natural level, are erected in blocks, the largest block covering a space of solid glass surface of about 200x100 feet. This block is composed of thirteen parallel sections, the continuity of the beds being broken only by an openwork of supporting posts and foot walks. The width of the houses in this block is sixteen feet, elevation at the ridge eight feet, the ridge timbers being supported by a line of light center posts, the side sills by heavy posts four feet high and five feet apart. These posts rest on brick foundations. At one end of the line of houses is a glass-roofed cross-section covering a footwalk of thirty inches, and covering also a plant bench forty inches wide set against the wall; on this bench may be raised any of the small crops. Under the bench mushrooms are successfully grown, the light being excluded by cloths hanging in front and reaching to the ground, the mushroom spawn pricked out on a level surface, the earth and manure mixture being first properly compounded, and upon the degree of its proper preparation much depends the measure of success.

The ventilation is, of course, a most important subject. As a rule, plants do not get enough of it, but of this experience alone can be the only guide. The glass is thick, 10x12, put on with oil and lead mixture, the panes lapping and fixed in place by S hooks. The glass selected is free from blisters. The cost of such houses is estimated at three dollars per running foot.

For houses where the operations are sufficiently extensive to warrant the employment of a night engineer, steam, as the heating agent, is found to be more efficient than hot water, as by steam perfect control of the temperature can be had, but, in houses so small as not to profitably sustain the expense of a night engineer, hot water is recommended; as the water well heated up at bed-time may, with banked fires in the furnace, be relied upon to sustain a safe temperature till morning.

The heating system in the houses under consideration is by four six-inch steam pipes passing through each house, of sixteen feet in width, such pipes carried about eight inches above the level of the surface beds. Protection from wind is a valuable factor in the economical heating of a forcing house, as in bleak situations more than double the coal is required than is consumed in sheltered situations. The plant beds are watered by a hose which is attached to a three-inch supply pipe running along the passage at one end of the houses.

The soil used in these houses is removed every year and spread in extensive chicken pens, where it is scratched over and worked up by the fowls, which exterminate all insect life, while at the same time fertilizing and ameliorating the mass. The plant beds, after being excavated, are filled in with earth from the chicken pens, where it has already been worked over by fowls. The manure used is finely decayed stable manure or compost, the elements of which are of little consequence, so that they be thoroughly decayed and in fine condition. Of course, the usual precautions are taken to keep in subjection lice and other insects. Fumigation by burning tobacco stems is cheap and effective if not overdone.

Three good paying crops raised in glass houses are considered a full success, often only two are really profitable. The rotation of crops is, first, lettuce, which, when removed, is followed by radish, and, when an inch high, if on the level, may have set out among it cauliflower plants. The variety of lettuce found most reliable is Boston Market, which has a good leaf and carries well; of radish for shipment, the Carmine Globe is of good form and color, though there is a large demand in Philadelphia for a small early white turnip radish. Of cauliflower, the extra early Erfurt is a quick and reliable variety. Other crops are grown in considerable breadth, water cress, parsley, French sorrel, mint and tomatoes, often bringing sixty to seventy-five cents per pound. The laborers required in a house covering a square of twenty thousand feet is from five to ten men.

The commercial gardener who has the capital and ability to carry on an extensive system of vegetable gardening under glass, thoughtfully secures a line of direct customers for his products by making contracts with hotels, restaurants and club houses, not depending upon the chance sales of commission merchants. Such contracts as referred to cannot be obtained by a small producer, as his crop is too limited and too transient to command the confidence of a large daily consumer who cannot afford to run any chances of supply.

The highest price obtained for head lettuce is generally in the month of March, when they sometimes bring seven dollars per one hundred. Small red radishes sell highest in January and February, when they often bring forty cents per one hundred, put up in bunches of twelve. Cauliflowers are most profitable in March and April, and they frequently bring fifty cents each. Of course, it is understood that all vegetables, especially those forced under glass, are in best condition immediately after pulling or cutting, but it may be profitable to know the maximum extent of time during the cool months, during which hothouse vegetables can be transported in satisfactory condition. This period for lettuce, cauliflower and radishes, from two to three days, provided they are carefully packed.

Plan No. 3. The style of construction of houses under system No. 3 is the design of a market gardener of Camden, N. J., Mr. Rodolphus Bingham, who has built a very cheap forcing house for vegetables, the framework of which any farmer can erect. The house may be single, or better, double. The sills are laid upon the natural earth thirteen feet apart, kept from spreading by stakes driven on the outside, the rafters and ridge erected, the sash laid on, and the work is done, except placing boiler with furnace and fitting hot water pipes. The advantages claimed by Mr. Bingham for this plan are:

First—A saving in cost of construction by doing away with all supporting posts or walls.

Second—A saving of heat by placing the furnace

and boiler in a pit in the center of the house, so that all radiated heat may be utilized.

Third—Carrying the smoke flues from the furnace the entire length of the house, and beneath one of the beds if the house be a double one; then carrying the smoke beneath the middle sill, provided the length is not more than one hundred feet in each direction, so as to get all the heat out of the smoke which otherwise would pass out of the stack.

Fourth—By keeping the glass down near the beds the volume of air to be heated may be reduced to a minimum.

Fifth—By carrying hot water pipes, in large air flues, twelve or fourteen inches below the surface of the plant beds, the tops of the flues planked over with open joints, so that a large volume of warmed air may pass upward through the soil. By the several plans of underground heating Mr. Bingham claims that fifty per cent. of the heat wasted in other houses is saved, and in the health of the plant is found a practical application of the rule relating to human hygiene—that to most fully preserve health it is best to keep the "feet warm and the head cool."

For ventilation, one or all the outside sashes may be pulled down, or off, that on warm days the plants may be literally turned out of doors to free air and direct sunshine. The rafters and caps are of original design, and the entire arrangement is claimed as a combination of many of the best principles of forcing house construction. The joints are so made as to be very thoroughly air tight. The surface of the beds is nearer the glass than in other plant houses, the roof structure being set down upon the natural surface of the earth; the house, in fact, being nothing but a roof or combination of roofs, the paths under the ridge being excavated twenty-four inches deep in the solid earth, the plant beds being upon the surface near the glass, at a convenient distance for working, and all within an arms length.

The mechanical work, except boiler-setting and pipe-fitting, may all be completed in the sash factory, and readily set up or taken down by any farmer. The beds are five feet six inches wide. The entire structure map be taken apart in summer and stored away. In the autumn the sills may be laid, the roof-frame erected, the sash put on, and the house used for plants till early spring, when the beds may be set full with cauliflowers, tomato or egg plant, and six weeks earlier than would be safe outside, and after all danger of frost is past, the sash, caps and rafters may be removed, and the crops cultivated and matured far in advance of any in the garden.

Mr. Bingham has now two houses 26x250 feet which he erected in the middle of January over ground frozen seven inches deep, in which he set many thousands of plants as fast as the ground was thawed. These he has carried through severe weather, ranging down to zero, with less than one-half in cost of coal used in other houses of the same surface. From the 1st to the 9th and from the 13th to the 15th of February, when the thermometer ranged down as low as 20° Fahrenheit at sunrise, he had no fire in the furnace, the warmth in the ground, with the sunlight, being sufficient to keep the plants growing and in healthy condition. Such a house is more simple to work than more expensive structures, and costs 30 per cent. less to build and requires but 50 per cent. of the heating power.

Farmers who have ordinary hotbed sashes may use them on the frame of such a house, but, as a rule, such sashes are made of glass far too small, the many bars and joints arresting too much sunlight. The best modern sashes are made with glass not less than 12x16 inches. The sash bars should be narrow, the glass not put in with putty but with white lead and oil mixed to a syrupy consistency and applied with an oil can. Those who use long broad glass will all testify to the very great advantage of doing away with all possible obstructions to light.

In the most rudimentary work as well as in higher class gardening, a house of this design will be found practical for efficiency, cheapness, easy heating, and, to the farmer accustomed to the inclement work of managing winter and spring hotbeds, it will be found to save much uncomfortable exposure. The maximum of elevation is six and one-half feet from the bottom of the footwalk, which is a trench two feet deep cut out of the solid earth, this reducing the volume of air to be heated, as many houses have too much overhead space, and therefore are very expensive to heat.

Novices in gardening under glass cannot expect to immediately gain a knowledge of the processes practiced by professional men who have given years of close study to the development of the best methods of forcing plants. In order to reap the largest returns from vegetable forcing houses the beds should be ready to plant by the end of September, not later than the first week in October. The soil for the beds should be naturally of good texture, and incorporated with a liberal amount of short, well-rotted stable manure that has been composted and thoroughly worked over, so that the coarser fiber of the straw or litter has disappeared. To get this condition, which is very essential, the manure will have to be in a fermenting heap for nine to twelve months before it is thoroughly fit to use. Garden soil, or old sods, still better, a good percentage of peat, mixed in with the manure, will add to its value for the purposed needed. Gardeners located near large cities obtain street sweepings from the streets where horses stand; this they mix in with the short stable manure, the mass forming, when thoroughly decomposed, a rich black mold, an excellent fertilizer. Some gardeners make use of a light application of superphosphate of lime and of nitrogenous fertilizer, as dried meat and blood, before planting the beds. But the main reliance is best placed upon the compost heap. Those who water with enriched water find one ounce of sulphate of ammonia to five gallons of water to be an excellent application for lettuce, while for radishes, two ounces of dried blood to five gallons of water produce the best results. Before planting, the soil on the beds should be worked over and pulverized, the surface made smooth and level. Lettuce is generally the first crop, and set with a dibble at seven to eight inches apart each way. This part of the operation requires no great skill, outside of getting the lines straight and setting the plants at proper depth and at proper distances apart, the lines being parallel to each other in both directions. This is essential, so that at times when the surface crusts, it can be loosened each way by the use of small scuffle hoes. This operation may be found necessary two or three times during the growth of the plants.

Practical gardeners know that none of the curled-leaved varieties of lettuce will stand forcing under glass. This is so well understood that those having any experience never plant any of the curled sorts in a vegetable forcing house. The varieties which will succeed best for these purposes are Forcing, Tennis Ball, Silver Ball, Bloomsdale Reliable, Boston Market and Big Boston. The first two kinds are compact in growth, while all make good heads under glass, and they are, without doubt, the most profitable sorts to grow. The experienced gardener purchases his seeds only from seed merchants of established reputation.

To secure plants for the first crop the seed should be sown in a sheltered space in the garden, say six weeks before the time for planting, August 15th or September 1st, for example. For the second and third crops the seed may be sown under glass in a corner of one of the houses a month before the plants are wanted for setting out. It is always a safe plan to sow an abundance of seed, for very often a portion of the plants in the seed bed meet with some mishap, cutting the supply short when it is too late to replenish the stock in good time. If the houses are kept at the proper temperature, the first crop planted, say October 1st, will be ready for market in seven to eight weeks from the time of planting. This will give an abundance of time to raise three crops of lettuce between October 1st and the latter part of March. This is allowing considerable margin for harvesting each crop, and to make the necessary preparations for planting. This preparation of the beds for the second and third crops is similar to the first, with the exception that, if manure is applied freely for the first, the soil will be rich enough to mature the three crops without any addition, except, perhaps, a little ammoniacal fertilizer as a stimulant. This should be scattered on and raked in during the preparation for the second and third crops. The rapid and uniform growth of lettuce depends largely on the quality of the soil in which it is set, and the judicious management of the house, in heating and watering. There is no use in starting a crop under glass with poor, hungry soil; there should be no doubt on this question of fertility, for without it all efforts at culture will fail. If the gardener has a number of forcing houses under his control, he should not plant too much of one kind at a time, but at intervals of one or two weeks, so that his whole crop will not mature at the same time, as it throws too much work upon him at once, and possibly at an unprofitable period. Instead of a third crop of lettuce, some gardeners sow a crop of radishes. As a rule, the receipts from a crop of radishes will amount to about the same as from a third crop of lettuce, which, of course, is always less than the first or second crop.

A week or two before the last crop of lettuce is ready for market, hills for cucumbers may be made six to eight feet apart in the beds, and the seeds planted. The lettuce is out of the way long before the cucumbers begin to run and need room. Cucumbers planted in this manner come into market at the same time others arrive from Florida and Charlestown. The forced cucumbers sell freely for twice as much as those coming from the South, being fresh and crisp, while the others are not. When the cucumbers are taken off, the houses are given rest for the balance of the summer, unless the market is such as to warrant those usually less profitable crops, such as asparagus, egg plant, tomatoes, rhubarb, parsley, sorrel, chives and strawberries.

Aphis, or Green Fly.—Among the most serious annoyances to the indoor gardener is the "green fly." Fumigating with tobacco leaves is the most general remedy. This operation has to be repeated twice a week as long as any flies remain. The most simple, and an effective method of fumigating, is to have a number of small sheet iron cones, from fifteen to eighteen inches high, and eight to ten inches in diameter, each having a grate near the bottom, an opening to give draft, and a damper to regulate the draft. In each place a charge of damp tobacco stems and wood shavings, and set them in different parts of the house, igniting all at the same time. This will be found the best and most effectual way to apply the tobacco, using about two pounds of dry tobacco to every one thousand feet of glass.

Profits from Forcing Houses.—The profits from this branch of market gardening depend largely upon the skill and intelligence of the gardener. The first and second crops of lettuce, if planted at the dates named, and well grown, with crisp, solid heads, may sell at wholesale at from seventy-five cents to a dollar a dozen, or from four to five dollars a barrel. The third crop sells for less, say from fifty to seventy-five cents a dozen. Clean, perforated barrels are best for shipping lettuce, and when carefully packed the lettuce will keep fresh for a week. There are times when general business is dull and prices fall below these figures, and, on the other hand, times when there is a good demand; then prices are higher than those named.

The house under system No. 4 may be of the same construction as either Nos. 1, 2 and 3, but differs from them in being without any apparatus for heating. It may, therefore, be properly termed a sun house. It is an improvement upon the "cold frame" long used for growing vegetables for early winter and spring use. By the old system of cold frames, only one crop of lettuce could be grown. The plants were set late in autumn, and the crop so handled as to be ready for market early the following spring, a month or six weeks before crops are produced in the open garden. But now, in sun houses, modern practical gardeners have a new and improved method of raising lettuce under glass without artificial heat. This new method, although more expensive for the first outlay and construction, has, after several years of experience, proved to be more certain and profitable in the long run than houses provided with artificial heat, and it is asserted, by those who have such houses in full operation, that, considering the difference in the first cost, they are more profitable than those equipped with the most modern heating apparatus. In these houses three crops of lettuce can be grown in a season, while with those furnished with artificial heat only two, often only one, additional crop can be grown with profit.

Sun houses may be built on the same plan and of the same dimensions as any of the forcing houses described, the only difference being that there is no method of heating introduced, and that the plant beds are all on solid earth, never on raised benches; the only expense over construction being the introduction of labor-saving methods for watering with rubber hose. This watering apparatus may be identical with that recommended for forcing houses.

Before setting out lettuce, of course it will be necessary to have the soil in the beds worked up to a rich and mellow condition. Every practical gardener knows full well that this is of the utmost importance to insure success; if neglected, or but half done, failure is almost certain to follow. To the intelligent market gardener this hint is superfluous, but it is a subject of primary importance to be impressed upon the mind of the beginner. The same preparation and proportion of soil and manure recommended for beds in the forcing house should be used for plant beds in sun houses.

Market gardeners, as a class, are just awakening to the fact that there is more money to be made in working these sun houses than the more expensive heated houses, furnished with modern heating furnaces, boilers and pipes. Owing to this fact, a very large number of sun houses have been built during the last three or four years in the vicinity of Philadelphia. It seems, also, needless to say that these houses are profitable, and in every respect more desirable than the old-fashioned cold frames or boxes. Truckers, or market gardeners, operating on the northern line of the cotton belt will, no doubt, find in that comparatively mild section a favorable location for sun houses, while, at the same time, near enough to the northern cities to be able to deliver their vegetables in good condition.

CHAPTER XVIII.

Celery.

The best soil for celery is muck. Sandy loam is also very good, but requires heavy fertilizing, as celery is a rank feeder. A swamp, well drained and in good tilth, will grow strong celery. Muck soil, that will grow a crop of onions or potatoes, will grow a succeeding crop of celery the same season. On sandy loam the same thing can be done, with the addition of a good dressing of stable manure. Celery is usually grown as a *second crop*, after early peas, beets, onions, early potatoes, turnips, and sometimes cabbage; the ground for these crops should always be heavily dressed the previous autumn with good barnyard manure. Celery plants are often set out on potato ground before the potatoes are dug, every third row of the potatoes being omitted. The cultivation of the ground for potatoes is good preparation for celery. In hoeing, a trench is made at the place of the omitted rows, in which—about the middle—a double row of celery plants is set. Market gardeners generally confine themselves to growing one or two varieties proven to be profitable and salable, their object being to put on the market an article pleasing to the eye, tender, crisp and solid. The dwarf sorts are now more extensively raised than the large, for the reason that, in quality, they are every way as good, and require less field space, besides being easier to work.

Years ago, under the laborious and expensive method of cultivation, celery was not a very profitable crop; but within the past twenty years the acreage and profits have increased, under the new and improved system of "flat culture," the old method of deep trenching having been discarded. A brief description, in way of history, will suffice for the old system, which enlightened gardeners now never follow:

The seed was sown in a hotbed in March, and the plants pricked out into temporary beds before final transplanting to give them greater strength. In June and July, as needed for successive crops, trenches were dug five feet apart, about eight to ten and fifteen inches wide. The soil in the bottom of each trench was thoroughly and deeply mixed with manure forked in. The plants were set out in the deep trenches at distances of five to six inches apart in the row. The earthing up was much the same as now practiced.

There can be no fixed date for sowing, which is now done in the open garden or field, the time depending upon the state of the season and location of the planter. Usually, in the latitude of Philadelphia, the ground is fit to receive the seed about April 1st. There need be no particular hurry to get it in very early, except to get the start of weeds and the benefit of spring showers. The seed germinates slowly, is one of the smallest the gardener uses, and the plant, at the beginning, is a frail, tiny little thing. Even small lumps of earth resting upon seeds or plants, at this stage, will certainly retard, if not effectually prevent, growth. For these reasons the preparation of the ground, previous to sowing, should be done in a more thorough manner than for larger seeds. The soil should be rich from heavy manuring the previous year, or from thoroughly rotted dung, spread over the land to the depth of about an inch.

The work of preparation and sowing of a celery bed is best done at a time when all the operations will be completed in one day, the manure being spread and worked under before the sun has dried it, and the seed put in while the earth is in that state of moisture immediately following plowing. It is best sown in rows, a quarter of an inch deep and ten inches apart, and distributed thinly. If the weather is damp the seed should not be covered; if dry, the bed should be gently patted with a piece of board, to solidify the soil and hasten germination. If sown in beds broadcast, the seed should be mixed with dry sand in the ratio of one to five, facilitating evenness of distribution. Transplant when three inches high. When in rows, as soon as the young plants appear, cultivate between the rows with a narrow garden rake at least twice a week, weeds or no weeds. When well established, the plants should be thinned to one or two inches, or all taken up and transplanted in rows ten inches apart, two inches between the plants.

The ground, having been heavily manured in the spring for early crops of cabbages and other vegetables, still contains a large percentage of plant food, which is available for celery at the time of transplanting. In gardens in the highest state of cultivation an extra manuring is not necessary, for, although celery is a rank feeder, there is generally enough fertilizing matter left from the preceding manuring to grow the crop. When the celery field is plowed and harrowed thorougly, the rows should be marked out; for the large kinds five feet apart, for the dwarf three feet, and for that portion of the crop which is to be stored in trenches for winter use, distances are narrowed about a foot, as this celery will not be earthed up.

In small fields the rows are best made by stretching a cord across the field. A stick is then drawn along the line to mark the row, or, if the ground is in nice order, the line may be patted with a spade, the impression of the line being left in the soil. On large fields the marking out is best done with a horse marker or sled. A marker can be made to draw three rows at a time, teeth or runners V-shaped, three feet long, twelve inches deep, and four or five inches wide at the rear end. The driver rides, and the rows, when opened, are about two inches deep and four inches wide.

Before a crop of celery can be expected to grow luxuriantly, the land must be prepared thoroughly. This previous cultivation for celery must include deep culture. Celery roots demand plenty of room. The writer has walked over a celery field after potatoes, where plants had been set out four weeks, and, by digging down twelve inches, found celery roots filling all the soil. Get the cultivation deep; carry the manure along and keep weeds out of sight, and, where possible, irrigate during dry seasons.

Transplanting may be done in the latter part of June for early crops, but celery grown in market gardens as a second crop is not usually put in until the ground is entirely cleared of the preceding crops. The cabbages and other vegetables being disposed of early in July, the celery planting can then begin. It is not desirable to forward celery for marketing in the early autumn, because there is not much demand for it until poultry appears in market. About the 15th of July to middle of August is usually, in the latitude of Philadelphia, the season for transplanting out in the field; but the first weeks of July give best results, the plants having the help of July rains in their new position, while later setting must sometimes be followed by irrigation.

The transplanting may be all done at once, or in two or three successive crops. In midsummer there is, as a rule, but little rain, while wet weather is desirable, for the planting can be not only better done in rainy weather, but the plants need the excess of moisture to enable them to take root during a season of heat. Every arrangement should, therefore, be made beforehand, so that a seasonable rain may be taken advantage of. In fact, the whole business requires, and should receive, much thought and judicious management, and all the operations should be conducted in a thoroughly systematic manner.

When transplanting time is decided upon the plants have to be dug with spade or trowel, and trimmed, root and top, before they are set out. The digging and trimming is an operation taking time, and, before planting begins, enough plants must be got ready to start the planters, and the work of trimming keep pace with the planting. Have ready a large pail of mud, earth and water, stirred to the consistency of cream; in this dip the roots, using only large strong plants. Drop the plants in the freshly opened row, six inches apart. If the ground be in good friable condition, and moist, a quick man following a boy to drop, will set out eight thousand plants a day and do it well. One quick movement of the two hands will draw moist earth about the roots of a plant lying in the row, and, at the same time, set it upright. Another brush of the hands will cover this moist earth with loose, dry earth, to level the ground. Attention is called, at this point, to double rows, which are grown at less expense than two distinct single rows. Double row culture gives good results, as to the quantity of product, affording place for double the amount on an acre, but, of course, is never to be undertaken except in ground fully able in richness to develop such a crop. In double rows the plants are set six inches apart, and the two rows six inches distant from each other, with four feet between each set of rows. Thus, in an acre of 43,560 square feet, with equal sides, there is place for fifty-two row spaces, and each single row will contain 416 plants; a double row 832.; 832x52= 43,264 plants per acre, set as above described. On muck, two acres, the writer has known 75,000 celery plants grown successfully year after year. Hot south and west winds have to be guarded against, because, under their influence, moisture disappears from the soil as rapidly as from a burning brick kiln, and all surface-rooted vegetation comes to a complete standstill. To guard against injurious winds a tight board fence eight feet high can be erected with profit. The preparation of celery ground should always include some plan for providing moisture, especially if in a section of country where dry weather prevails in August.

A row of tanks, each thirty-six inches wide, thirty inches deep and fourteen feet long stands at the head or most elevated portion of a profitable celery garden, known to the writer. The tanks are connected at the ends by short tin spouts. They are set on trestles, the first twenty inches above the ground, the second two inches lower, and so on to the last. A windwill, erected over a large well close by, pumps water into the highest tank, and, when full, it overflows into the next, and on, until all are full. On the side of each tank, close to the bottom, a one and a half inch hole is bored opposite each row of celery, and tight plugs inserted. When the celery begins to show signs of suffering, for want of moisture, the windmill is set to work and the tanks filled. At sunset the plugs are knocked out, the waters gush forth, striking on pieces of board, and flow down the celery trenches. This is repeated the following evening. Every third evening is passed and the harrow run between the rows. Irrigation is continued while the drouth lasts, and the celery invariably makes a splendid growth.

About the 10th of September begins the handling of that portion of the crop intended for the early market. One man drawing the loose soil toward the plants with a hoe, another grasping the entire plant with his right hand, holding it straight up, the stalks close together, drawing the earth against it with his left, then holding the plant in his left hand, packing the earth around it with his right. With a little practice, this operation is performed very rapidly. A double shovel plow may be profitably run between the rows a few times, to loosen up the soil, which is drawn toward the plants as required. The finishing touch is given with the spade, the earth being banked clear to the top of the plants.

That part of the crop intended for the winter market is handled the same as the other, but is earthed up *only* with the hoe, the blanching being done in the trenches in which it is stored for winter. In handling and earthing up, the main point is to keep the stalks of the plant so close together that no soil can get between them. After this "handling" is done, the plants are left to grow two weeks, and are then further earthed up. The bank must be made broad at the base, and the side sloped up, so that they will not cave or slide. As the plants grow higher the earth is dug from the center of the row with a spade, and banked up against the celery. The celery will be blanched in about four weeks. Celery can be successfully blanched in the field, between boards, by adopting the following process: Tie up the plants with yarn or other convenient material, and, taking common boards twelve inches wide, place them on opposite sides of the row three inches apart, fasten them there with stout pegs driven on the outside of each board. The celery leaves projecting out of the top will exclude the light, and the stems become white and remain free from rust. The plan is the same as is pursued in blanching endive, sea kale and asparagus. Under this system the plants should stand close in the rows, say six inches, and the rows may be closer than where banking is practiced, say three feet. Celery should not be banked up while the stalks are wet with rain or dew. A large grower, well known to the writer, cultivates flat into August, then banks at the rate of five thousand per man per single day's work, and once again early in September, then covers it from frost in the row or removes it to the trench or other storing place. This work must be well done, even if it is rapidly done, but practice makes light fingers. Boys must be watched, or, better, not employed; as the strength of a mature hand is needed. After the first banking, and new stalks start, one will soon learn to have a few rows ripe and ready for market or home use every day, until cold weather requires the removal of the plants to the storing place.

Storing trenches should only be dug in dry soil, well underdrained, or where water does not stand. These trenches are made the width of a spade, and as deep as the celery is high. Just before frost the celery is dug up and packed in an upright position in these trenches. No covering is put on until cold weather sets in. It will stand light frosts. Finally the trench is covered with hay, or other litter, the earth rounded up along and over the trench. In the latitude of Philadelphia celery is stored away in this way, beginning the last of October, and finishing by November 15th. The first in, is first blanched; the last keeps till February and March. A covering of boards over the litter will keep the rain off, and is to be recommended. The winter storage of celery is a matter of the deepest importance, as, if not properly done, all previous efforts go for nothing. The novice will do best by trying several systems, and subsequently adhering to that which proves the best in his climate.

Celery can be stored by burying in the row where it grew, by removing to trenches, to boxes in the cellar, or to a temporary pit specially prepared for large quantities. The first method is often practiced with double rows in muck ground, and during warm winters has proved quite successful. The object of any method is to protect from frost, and maintain plant life, for the celery is most healthy when it continues to grow, or, at least, draw moisture through its roots, till it is marketed. It is an easy matter to secure growth in good ground, with sunshine and wind and rain, but with the coming of frost the celery must be removed to close quarters. If buried in the row it must be where water will not collect, but where good drainage can be relied upon. With the stalks banked their entire length, a few leaves are left as long as possible exposed, but finally these are covered with straw or manure, at first lightly, then heavily, and then again very heavily, so as to shut out hard frost for a long period. This can be managed so as to allow the celery to be taken out for use from the under side in very cold weather. This method has risks; one must assume them and trust each night's cold will not freeze the celery, or a day's warmth smother it under too much covering. Another way is to dig a trench one or two feet wide, as deep as the stalks, and on loose earth, scattered in the bottom, place the celery as close together as possible, wetting the earth about the roots. Begin to cover with manure, and increase with frost. But now the celery must be watched, every week it must be examined. If, after a time, leaves lose their green color, wet the roots without wetting the stalks, and watch for rust, dark brown spots, a fungus growth, quick to spread throughout the whole mass of plants. Such stalks must be immediately removed and sent to market; if allowed to remain they will entirely decay and breed disease among all the rest. Absolute protection is claimed against fungus growth by spraying the celery plants with Bordeaux mixture every second day during four weeks preceding their storage. A method of winter storage, by which the risks are largely removed, is to provide boxes twelve inches deep, fill them half full of good earth, in which set out the celery, closely packed, the first week of October, and carry the boxes into the cellar. If there be room enough the cellar can contain many boxes and many thousand plants. Have the earth moist in the boxes, and watch for the need of water; get water in at the roots, a little only at a time, to promote growth. The stalks will stand high up about the sides of the boxes, and as the nights become cooler the cellar doors must be closed. Carefully pull out any dead or dying stalks, and watch for rust, also. In this manner celery is easily kept, and the method is advised for the small operator.

The last method is that of a temporary outdoor cellar, built for the purpose, in or near the celery ground. A sort of pit or dug-out is made on dry upland, twenty-four feet wide, and as long as needed, each foot in length holding one thousand celery plants. Dig the sides straight down, and cover with sixteen-foot boards for a roof, meeting over the center. Provide fine earth in the bottom and set out the celery just as described for cellar boxes, then water the roots as may be needed. The structure must be made frost proof. Examine the whole stock every week. A storm door is required at the entrance, also a window with shutter to admit light.

If the distance is short and the celery carried in wagons, it can be placed in barrels, the bunches resting on the roots, the tops upright. Some precaution against frost is necessary. Chests are made for packing purposes, and lined with straw. The bunches are carefully protected from bruising by skillful packing.

As celery is generally a second crop, the cost is reduced to a minimum. It is planted and cultivated at a season when other things are not demanding much attention, and the crop fills a gap in the garden, when, if not grown, the land might be unprofitable. But the preparation for market, if time is considered, costs nearly as much as the growing. Enough plants may be sold, in planting season, to pay for seed and summer cultivation—that is, in some gardens. These things taken into consideration, the cost is probably two hundred dollars per acre. The cost of the crop varies, rarely being the same two successive years. Manure is comparatively cheap, but labor is dear.

Celery has been grown and marketed for one dollar and fifty cents per thousand plants, but the explanation must be added that only in rare instances of exceeding good fortune has this been done—where, from the seed to the selling, everything was remarkably cheap, labor at twenty-five to forty cents per day, by German women, who had become, by long practice, expert at the work. The safer figure to give is from fifteen to twenty dollars per thousand, especially for amateur efforts, and, while writing, distant growers are offering celery ready for shipment at the station for sixteen dollars per thousand. The reader can estimate for himself how small the margin of profit may be. For the rare instance: It is claimed, by one man, that he prepared, in one day, three muck beds, and sowed three dollars' worth of seed; it gave one hundred thousand plants, from which seventy-five thousand were selected. With a boy to drop the plants in the row, and a woman to set them out, fifteen such couples, with one man to dig plants from the bed, will set out seventy-five thousand in muck in one day. This, it is claimed, has been done repeatedly. Banking is done at the same rate; so that after the second banking the celery has cost less than seventy cents per thousand. A grower, who had sold seventy-five thousand, stated he did not think the crop had cost him one hundred dollars on his muck ground.

On sandy loam the cost is much greater, and the yield less bulky. Heavy manuring, frequent cultivation and much less rapid handling of plants in such ground, change the figures. From some grounds the writer has seen celery plants, each having fifty stalks by actual count. Such vigorous growth takes the lead in the market and fills the purse, but the average celery plant only numbers five to eight stalks. When one has, by long experience, and the use of proper seed, learned to grow such thrifty plants, their relative cost will be small. To prepare a muck field from the rough swamp is sometimes very costly, but on such ground celery grows luxuriantly with a minimum of cultivation, and the markets of the country are most largely supplied from such sources. Plants have been grown for three cents per thousand, and have been set out for fifteen cents, but the average price, if one buys plants, is two to three dollars per thousand, and in other than muck ground the setting out costs as much more. The amateur must grow celery one year, at least, to learn how, and to find whether it can be made profitable on his ground and in his market. The work may be done at less expense than the following estimate:

Interest on $150 @ 10%, $15. Manure, 40 loads @ $2=$80	$95.00
Plowing, harrowing and marketing, 1 man and team 1 day	3.00
Planting, 1 man 4 days @ $1.50=$6; cultivating, 1 man and horse 3 days @ 2$, $6	12.00
Hoeing twice, 1 man 3 days @ $1.50=$4.50; handling or tying, 1 man 10 days @ $1.50=$15	19.50
Banking, 1 man 15 days @ $1.50=$22.50; trenching, $10; water and watering, $6	38.50
13,000 plants @ $5=$65; preparing for market, $40	105.00
Total cost for one acre	$273.00

In preparing for market, the outside green leaves should be removed, leaving none but the blanched or edible part, with its green tops, roots nicely trimmed off and washed. Pack in neat round bunches of twelve stalks each, tied tightly at top and bottom; or inquire what is most favored in each market, and tie up in the acceptable form; don't attempt to develop many new ideas. For some distant markets it will pay to wrap each stalk separately in brown straw paper, and pack in boxes with slatted top. Any rusty or decayed spots on the celery can be quickly removed with a sharp, thin-bladed knife, which greatly improves its appearance. Prices range from twenty-five cents to two dollars per dozen, according to size and quality. Good celery will average eight cents per stalk, or, in round numbers, one thousand dollars per acre. Frequently the whole of the expense of manure can be covered by raising a spring crop on the ground, before planting the celery.

As an example of profitable celery culture, it may be cited that on a certain farm three hundred bushels of early potatoes were grown one season on two acres of muck ground, and brought one dollar per bushel; five thousand dozen celery were set out just before digging the potatoes, and became well rooted in the shade of the potato vines. The celery sold was shipped in many directions, and retailed at eight and ten cents per bunch. The celery brought the grower seventeen hundred and fifty dollars, and the crop cost him less than one hundred dollars as it left his hands.

CHAPTER XIX.

Onion Culture.

A strong, deep, rich, loamy soil is most suitable for an onion crop, and where very large bulbs are desired, it is indispensable. New land is especially adapted for the growth of onions. On ground of this character they can be raised at less than one-half the ordinary cost, little or no manure being necessary, and it is usually nearly free from weeds. Very dry, light or sandy soil is unfit for this high-feeding crop. The chief reason why so many are not successful in raising onions, is because they do not attach enough importance to the selection of their seeds; they start wrong, by buying cheap seed. This not only lessens, or loses the crop, but is a source of vexation, extending through the entire season.

No previous preparation is required with virgin soil. If old ground is to be used, manure heavily and plant to corn; cultivate thoroughly four or five times; do not permit weeds to go to seed; go through the field after the last cultivation of the corn; cut off the weeds, carrying away all likely to ripen seed, keeping a sharp lookout for purslane. Cut the corn early, and plow deeply in the fall.

As a manure for onions, well-rotted stable dung is the best. Artificial manures are uncertain, especially in dry seasons. Stable manure reserved for an onion crop, should be stacked up in summer, and left until autumn for processes of fermentation to fit the material as a plant food, and late in the fall it should be spread evenly, and twenty to twenty-five loads to the acre, and immediately plowed under. When possible, the ground should always be plowed in the autumn, again in the spring, and harrowed until the ground is thoroughly pulverized. No pains in tillage should be spared.

Various growers succeed best with different varieties, as have proved best adapted to their respective soils and markets. Among well established varieties there are the Yellow Globe Danvers, Extra Early Red, Large Red Wethersfield, Red Globe, White and Yellow Globe, Strasburg and Silver Skin.

Red Globe has the color and general quality of the Large Red Wethersfield, is round, is as hardy, keeps well, and rivals it in weight of crop.

Extra Early Red is a selection from Large Red Wethersfield, which, in color and form, it closely resembles. It is the earliest of all red onions, close grained, mild, a good keeper, and two or three weeks earlier than the Large Red. It is liable to degenerate, or revert to the Wethersfield, unless very careful selections of bulbs are made for seed, and the experienced grower will only buy this from experienced and trusted dealers.

Large Red Wethersfield is a broad, flat onion, bulbs often growing to five inches in diameter, and two and a half in depth, skin purplish-red, flesh purplish-white, moderately fine-grained and of strong flavor. There are several types of Wethersfield, some early, some medium, others late; the early form is best.

Yellow Globe Danvers, of the pure type, is inclined to be half globular in form, that is to say, flat on the bottom and round on top; it is above medium size, skin yellowish-brown, growing dark by age, flesh white, sugary, comparatively mild and well flavored, and exceedingly productive. There is a form of so called Yellow Danvers known as Flat Danvers, somewhat resembling the Strasburg.

Silver Skin produces bulbs medium in size, flattened, average specimens three inches in diameter, and one and a half to two inches thick; neck small, skin silvery white, after removal of outer envelope, top of bulb often veined and clouded with green, while that portion below ground is usually clear white. Flesh white, fine grained, and quite mild in flavor.

Yellow Strasburg is an old variety, still of high repute on account of its long keeping qualities and mild flavor. The bulb is somewhat larger than that of the Silver Skin, the flesh being equally white. It is the variety from which the best sets are grown.

Among other varieties not so well known are the Extra Early Yellow, the earliest of that color; Extra Early Pearl, the earliest white; Autumn White Wax, a choice early waxy variety, Bermuda White and Red.

Small patches of onion may be sown by hand, or through a long tin tube. Large breadths should be sown by a garden seed drill. Such can be purchased according to design at from five to seven dollars cash. There is no perfect seed-drill; all have faults. Possibly the Keeler is now the best form. It is light and easy to run, and distributes the seed evenly. The seed is best drilled in straight rows, one foot apart, six pounds of seed being sown to the acre. One acre can be sown in four hours with the Keeler drill, machine, weather, land and man in perfect working order. The seed should not be buried over one-third of an inch deep, and lightly rolled in by the roller attached to the drill. After sowing, a wooden garden roller should be used to level and solidify the land.

The best time to drill onion seed is as soon as the frost is out of the ground, and the soil dry enough for preparation; then set all hands to work and rush it through. No matter if light spring frosts are not all passed, don't be afraid of after-freezing, it won't hurt the crops. The reason for early planting is obvious, when it is known that onion seed will germinate at a lower temperature than most other seeds, while weed seeds require a much higher temperature; consequently, the onions will make their appearance ten days before the weeds, enabling the gardener to commence early cultivation, and thus keep weeds in check. Fall plowing facilitates early spring preparation, making early drilling practicable.

Salt is sometimes broadcasted upon an onion field to destroy the onion maggot, and its application is believed to hasten the maturity of the crop. It seems to keep the soil from drying out. Near the sea coast seaweed or sea grass is used as a fertilizer for onions, maggots or weeds seldom injuring a salted crop. Two bushels of salt to the acre is sufficient, more is dangerous.

In the cultivation four hoeings and three weedings are usually necessary; the last weeding must be done before the bottoms begin to form, or before the middle of July, as they often "blast" if worked when forming bulbs, many of them failing to make bulbs, and becoming "scullions." The season for hoeing and weeding covers about two months. After July 20th the crop should be safely under way. One man can tend two acres, and have time to spare, but in the weeding time he will need a helper, as the whole field, be it large or small, must be cleaned within a few days, as, when weeding is necessary, it is always pressing. Hand hoeing and hand weeding is more efficient than work done with scuffle hoes, which do not do the work thoroughly. Flat hoeing is all that is necessary, no effort being made either to draw the dirt up to the onions, or away. Purslane is the most troublesome weed, usually appearing in abundance at the last weeding. It must be carried off in baskets or sacks. The time occupied in cultivating a crop of onions covers from two to three months.

In the latitude of Philadelphia harvesting is commenced about August 1st, or whenever two-thirds of the tops fall and begin to turn yellow; pull them by hand, when seasoned so that the juice cannot be squeezed from the neck, rake in heaps, and pull or cut the tops off. Place in heaps of twenty-five to thirty bushels each, on the field; cover with straw or tarpaulin, so as to keep dry. An itemized estimate of the cost of growing an acre of onions may be drawn as follows:

Use of land for twelve months	$20.00
Fertilizers applied	30.00
Fall plowing under	2.00
Spring preparation of ground	6.00
Cost of seed, six pounds @ $2	12.00
Drilling in	2.00
Top-dressing 1 barrel salt	1.00
Cost of cultivation until pulled	50.00
Topping 420 bushels onions	12.00
Hauling the same four miles	12.00
Total cost	$147.00
Cost per bushel	$ .35

Some onion growers have found it profitable to drill winter rye in September, and in March plow it down as a green manure, the mass of rye tops and root fibers furnishing a vast amount of plant food. Of course, after such a mat of green herbage is plowed under, it is absolutely necessary to roll it down hard, otherwise the cavities would cause a drying out of the soil, and the onion plants would suffer more than they gained.

There are several insects that do damage to the onion crop; one, a large white grub, eating the leaf stalks off beneath the surface of the ground. Manure is the best remedy, stimulating the plants to resist attacks. Another is a louse. The first indication of the presence of the louse is a moldy appearance of the stalks, and, upon examination with a glass, myriads of microscopic insects are revealed; these cause a stunted growth, if not resulting in death. The only remedy is to change the location of the next year's crop. Another destructive insect is a maggot, or small white worm, half to one-third of an inch long, which bores to the heart of the bulb in the latter part of the season. The writer has seen twenty in a single bulb. They are very troublesome in some years, and salt is believed to be the best remedy.

A fungus growth known as smut works great injury to the onion, and it sometimes appears on the plants even when but one or two inches high, and covers the green stems with a red and black substance, coming off upon workmen's shoes, implements and tools. The spores may thus be carried from one part of the field to another, or from one patch to another, and spread the disease, as every spore is capable of multiplying itself a thousand times. The only remedy for this disease is to change the location of the crop. All tools which have been used on a smutty onion field must be carefully washed and soaked in hot water, or they may re-establish the disease the succeeding year.

Duration of Culture on the Same Land.

Onions have been successfully raised on the same ground for twenty-five years in succession, but, of late years, the smut appears in about ten or twelve, and a new tract has to be taken more frequently than formerly.

The conditions of weather have much influence upon the onion crop. Extremely dry weather hinders the growth and makes the bulbs small; wet weather makes top, and delays ripening. The yield per acre varies with the cultivation, soil, and other circumstances, from 200 to 600 or 1,000 bushels; 350 bushels is considered an average yield. To illustrate the crop returns on large fields it may be interesting to note the results of seven years of culture by an expert grower:

	Acres.	Bushels.	Amount of Sales.
First year............	10	3,081	$1,059.00
Second year.........	10	3,124	981.00
Third year	10	3,159	894.00
Fourth year.........	10	3,660	639.00
Fifth year...........	11	2,890	1,656.00
Sixth year..........	11	3,053	2,344.00
Seventh year.	13	2,340	2,463.00
Total,	75	21,307	$10,036.00

The last year this grower cultivated thirteen acres; the aggregate yield was 2,340 bushels; the aggregate receipts were $2,463. The expenses were: Land, $130; gathering and marketing, $260; seed, $215; weeding, $275; manure, $50; preparing land and planting, $100; total expense, $1,030; net profits, $1,433. These figures also show an average of 284 bushels per acre, at an average price of forty-seven cents per bushel. Of course, there are records that far exceed this; for instance, last year, one and one-half acres, in one case, yielded 600 bushels, and brought $780, which must have given over $400 per acre net profit. The records above given show the result of a series of years where onions have been made a specialty. The example being taken of a man who began in poverty twenty-four years ago, to-day worth twenty-thousand dollars; but right here the reader must remember that at least sixty per cent. of his expenses came back in the shape of the earnings of himself and family.

Storing and Keeping Onions.

Half the secret of keeping onions well, is in housing them in a perfectly dry, sound condition. If they are to be disposed of before cold weather, they can be kept in any dry place where they can have plenty of air, the best place being on a loose floor, where the air can pass up through them.

Onions, to be preserved through winter, should be kept at a low temperature; if kept from actual freezing there is no danger of the temperature being too low; they should be kept dry, but if, by any chance, they get frozen, they should not be handled, merely covered and kept in the dark till the frost gradually leaves them. It is not the freezing which does the mischief, but moving them when frozen, and repeated thawing and withdrawing of frost. Wherever the essential conditions prevail of uniform low dry temperature, absence of light, and not too severe frost, they may be safely stored for winter. Above all things, moisture and heating in bulk should be guarded against. If these conditions are to be obtained in a cellar or a room above ground it may be used for winter storing. To avoid gathering moisture and heating, the bulbs should not be over two feet deep, better less. If too warm they grow and rot.

If they are to be kept through the winter, store them in a building with tight floors, under which the frost cannot get. On such a floor place scantling, upon which lay narrow boards, half an inch apart. Upon this drying floor build up a false partition one foot within the outside walls. Arranged in this way, they have a free circulation of air all around and under them.

When the temperature sinks to 20° it is well to fill in the space with straw, to stop the circulation of the cold air. They can be put in bins of this structure, from two to three feet deep. It is well to cover them over with hay or cornstalks sufficiently to protect them. If they should freeze, allow them to remain covered until completely thawed. Always handle them as carefully as apples, as even slight bruises cause them to mold or rot.

If there be no convenient structure suitable for the winter storage of onions in large quantity, one may be erected somewhat after the following plan: If to store twenty-five hundred bushels, erect a building twenty by thirty feet, with sixteen foot posts. It should stand the longest way north and south, with doors twelve feet wide, and high at each end. It should stand one foot from the ground, to admit of free circulation beneath, and be sided with matched boards lined with tarred paper. The floor should be of two-inch plank laid loose, and well supported. On this floor place blocks five feet apart, about five inches square, and twenty inches high; cover the floor with onions to the top of the blocks; place on these blocks timbers as large as three by four, and on these narrow boards for flooring one inch apart. On this floor place blocks, the same as before; fill in with onions, and so on as high as convenient. The blocks should be placed exactly over each other, as there will be a great weight on the lower boards. During the fall, when the weather is dry, open the doors at each end; this will give the air free circulation through them. They will bear the temperature down to twenty-five without injury. On the approach of cold weather, bank up the sides of the building to keep the frost from getting under. On warm, clear days, open the south doors. When it is desired to take out the onions commence at the south doors, by taking out the floor boards, and let them roll down to the first floor, for topping. If they get frozen they will generally come out sound, if left undisturbed till the frost is out.

The vitality of onion seed should always be carefully and thoroughly tested before sowing. The best way is to count out two or three samples of one hundred seeds each, and each separate sample place between two layers of cotton batting, resting on saucers, each containing a quarter inch of water. Put in a warm place, and keep water at same level. The seeds will sprout in a few days. Find the general average of percentage that will develop shoots of half an inch in length, and plant accordingly, assuming eighty-five per cent. a standard of highest vitality. If, with seed of eighty-five per cent. vitality, six pounds is proper to sow an acre, then with seed of only sixty per cent. vitality, nine pounds should be sown.

Be not deluded into the purchase of cheap seed, such is always questionable, always suspicious. In the first place, it may not grow at all, or not over fifty or sixty per cent.; and, secondly, and more damaging to the planter, it may be from common mixed stock, or prove late and staggy. This the grower only discovers after a loss of a season and expensive labor.

CHAPTER XX.

Mushroom Culture.

Before considering the subject of mushroom culture, it may be well to make some reference to this edible fungus, a genus much larger and more important as a food than generally supposed.

Dr. Badham, an English authority upon fungi, states that hundreds of tons of rich, wholesome food go to waste daily in England, because of ignorance and superstition.

In England there are, at least, forty species of edible mushrooms, and in the United States many hundreds. In the State of North Carolina alone, there are one hundred and twenty species of fungi, many of them obtainable over a season of nine months. Mountain and plain, valley and forest, are swarming with a profusion of nutritious food going to decay because of the ignorance of the public.

The soil for earth fungi and the wood for forest fungi, however, has much to do with flavor, as occasionally a most excellent variety proves to be unpalatable, and even offensive. Of forest or tree fungi, those growing on the mulberry and on the hickory are generally of the best flavor. Dr. Curtis, of South Carolina, is, perhaps, among Americans, the most venturesome in tasting wild fungi—beginning with a single mouthful, the next day two or three mouthfuls, and the next a full meal. It takes a braver man than he who first swallowed an oyster to make experiments like this for the benefit of botanical science. Though sick stomachs and some inflammation have frequently resulted from eating poisonous or unwholesome mushrooms, it is rare to hear of an authenticated record of death from such causes. Mushrooms, which are safe with some persons, often disagree with others; indeed, it seems the stomach may be educated to bear most noxious species, as there are records of highly poisonous varieties being eaten with impunity by mushroom tasters.

As before remarked, soil and circumstances cause fungi to assume different properties, and the novice, when uncertain as to the merit of an unrecognized species, will find it a good plan to try the new sort with great caution. In no garden process is there such contradictory practice as in mushroom culture, and, while generally considered a subject requiring much experience and skill, the diversified system of cultivation would seem to point to simplicity in the requirements. For instance, one successful grower will gather dry droppings from horses, and still further dry them, by spreading and frequent turning under cover. Another, equally successful as a grower, dispenses with all this trouble, taking stable dung fresh from the stalls, and mixing in a fourth part of good friable loam, piling it up for a week, then turning it over, and, if fermenting too strongly, adding more loam. This mixture, made into beds, is immediately charged with spawn.

A third grower takes his manure from an ordinary barnyard pile, and mixes in a fourth part of loam. Other growers will not use manure which has been fermenting, claiming that it will not produce mushrooms or a continuous crop. Another system is to take any good stable manure, and, removing sticks, stones, very long straw, or other coarse material, thoroughly mix and pile it in beds two feet high, thoroughly wet with water and stamp down. After a week or ten days, by which time it is quite hot, the pile is re-worked and left for another ten days, then it is in condition to be made into beds of the proper form and seeded. Sometimes four to six weeks are taken in the preparation of the manure, a leading object with most cultivators being to have it half decomposed, completely mixed, but not wet.

Mushroom Beds.—Possibly the best system for the amateur to pursue is to prepare his manure pile under cover, as in a shed or cellar, making his pile one-fourth loam and three-fourths of the best stable manure he can get, horse dung predominating, which should be piled first, to allow it to lose its fiercest heat, the loam helping to solidify the mixture. At spawning time the heat in the beds should range from sixty to eighty degrees, never above eighty-five. The heat of a bed may be reduced by opening holes with a crowbar, forcing it down to the very bottom. Of course the heat can be taken with a thermometer.

Spawn, as sold, may be looked upon as the *seed* used by mushroom growers, though it is a compounded article. That part of the mushroom appearing above ground, the part eaten and best known to the public, is what may be termed the flower and flower stem, the spores, or true seed, being produced upon the gills of the flower, which, under natural conditions, falling to the ground, germinate, and produce a fine underground mat of filaments. This underground growth being the true and perfect plant, the edible portion, as previously remarked, being the flower, or seed-bearing stem. It is not necessary here to describe how the spawn is made commercially, except to say that the English spawn comes in the form of light, dry, brittle bricks, while the French comes in the form of light flakes, resembling half-dried stable manure.

In seeding a bed with English spawn, one bushel should suffice for an area of one hundred square feet of surface, the bricks being broken into pieces the size of a walnut, and placed as hereinafter directed. The English spawn is the most reliable when the work is performed by amateurs. With the French spawn the flakes about the size of a silver dollar should be inserted edgeways into the beds, the outer edge just covered from sight. The operation of spawning is a very important one, the aim being to secure a uniform development of spawn filaments throughout the bed. When this growth of white fiber fails to appear after three weeks' time, the bed should be broken up and remade with an addition of one-third unfermented dung to give it heat again. Any good loamy soil is suitable for covering the beds after the spawn has started to grow. In Paris the beds are generally covered with two inches of white limestone soil, not through choice, but through convenience, and it does as well as anything else.

Location of Mushroom Beds.—Mushrooms may be grown in greenhouses any month of the year, and in graperies, pits, sheds, cellars and stables from April to October. They may also be grown on shelves or on the floor of any of these places. A novice in mushroom culture may, with little trouble and comparatively no expense, try his apprentice hand at cultivation in half barrels kept in a dark shed or cellar, and we would advise the following course for such a trial: Procure an empty whiskey or vinegar barrel with a firm head and bottom, and saw it in half. Pick out the best quality of unfermented stable manure obtainable, and thoroughly mix with one-fourth part good friable loam, pile the mass compactly, and tramp down and cover with ordinary stable manure for a blanket. At the end of a week remove the covering and turn the mixture, pile it up again and blanket for two or three days, then half fill the tubs or barrels with the manure. Upon the top surface lay pieces of spawn the size of a walnut at intervals of three inches apart, and add sufficient of the manure mixture to build up a cone-shaped elevation of twelve or fifteen inches. In ten days the spawn should have sprouted and filled the whole mass of manure with white thread-like filaments. When these are seen running through the entire pile, cover it with two inches of fine loam, through which the mushroom buttons will develop, and from which the cultivator should be able to get a fair supply covering a period of from two to four weeks.

Mushrooms in the Garden.—Near London and Paris considerable quantities of mushrooms are grown in the open garden. In London ordinary manure is used, and before it has time to heat is made into long narrow beds. When the temperature reaches eighty degrees it is seeded with spawn, covered with two inches of any good soil, and blanketed with mats or tarpaulins. In Paris, the outdoor cultivator generally lets the manure ferment, and after frequent and thorough working, makes beds thirty inches wide and two feet in height, which he covers with mats.

When the temperature falls to eighty degrees he spawns the bed, inserting pieces of spawn the size of a walnut, placing it in three lines, one near the bottom edge of the bed, the second ten inches up along the side, and the third ten inches above the second. He next covers with mats or cloth. After ten days, if the spawn has started, he covers with two inches of soil.

The writer had the pleasure, a few years ago, of visiting the mushroom caves of Paris, the extent of such cultivation being measured by the daily product of four tons of buttons. The work is done in the underground caverns and galleries of the old limestone quarries, from which was taken the stone to build the city.

The manure is mixed upon the surface, lowered in large buckets, and in the same manner returned to the surface for remaking. Of course, all the work has to be done by candle light, and, being done in narrow passages, the operation covers many miles; the beds of one French cultivator, if placed in single line, would reach about twenty-six miles. The beds rest upon the rock bottoms of the galleries, and are built in the form of a ridge, two to three feet wide and two feet high. The limestone formation beneath Paris seems to be more especially adapted to mushroom culture than the rock formation in many other districts, coal and iron, in the rock soil, for instance, preventing the best growth of the mushroom.

CHAPTER XXI.

Roots for Stock Feeding.

This chapter is written in the hope of diffusing information inducive to greater attention to a most valuable adjunct in husbandry, and, if more widely regarded, calculated to increase, not only the quantity, but the quality, of our food; the tender, luscious mutton of the English, being attributable not alone to their cooler climate, but to the turnip, and, we may add, other *succulent* roots on which the sheep are fed and fattened for the butcher.

The value of succulent food, in a hygienic or sanitary view, to man, and also to the animals which minister to his wants, need not be commented on. All who have paid attention to the subject agree in opinion as to its advantage, indeed, its absolute necessity, if the preservation of health be properly studied. The long winters of our country, which arrest vegetation, and oblige us to provide green food to be stored up in anticipation of the severe season, have necessarily induced inquiry and examination as to the class of vegetables which can be produced in greatest abundance, at least cost, with least exertion in the shortest space of time, and with least liability to failure of the crop under unfavorable atmospheric conditions, and also as of primary importance, with capability for preservation during winter months with slight danger of decay.

In Great Britain the culture of roots, round turnip, ruta baga and mangold has assumed gigantic importance, and it was estimated by writers on political economy, years ago, when the turnip product was much below the present, that its annual value was much more than the equivalent of the sum represented by the interest on the National debt, no inconsiderable amount, as everybody knows. Until the culture of roots, as they are termed, was extended and enlarged, in England, animal food was a luxury seldom within the reach of the operative classes, with whom vegetables and farinaceous compounds, not always of the best quality, were the main sources of sustenance. Now English fattened meats, even of American origin, are, in some shape, within reach of all, the factory operative, the mechanic, the tradesman and the landholder alike participating; and this change has grown out of, not so much national prosperity or increased wages, though both are indirectly affected, but the greater breadth of land in root culture.

American corn, with us the great meat producer, which has played so important a part in the development of our country, enabling the hardy emigrant from the older settlements to wrest the wilderness from the savage, and overcome the forest, is not grown in Great Britain or any portion of the north of Europe, there being known only as an import from our country. In this particular, Americans have an advantage impossible to estimate; but, great as it is, it should not lessen our exertion to produce succulent food, which augments the value of the farinaceous.

The principal succulent and saccharine roots, besides the turnip, raised for cattle feeding, are, it is almost unnecessary to observe, mainly comprised by the tribes of beets, carrots and parsnips. There are some others, but they are hardly of sufficient importance to occupy space in limited pages.

In this country the turnip and the ruta baga, or "Swede," as it is familiarly called, is more generally cultivated for stock-food than any other root—not that it is the best, but because it can be so readily grown, and at small cost. While beets, mangold, carrots, kohl rabbi and parsnip demand an entire season to mature, the turnip is of so quick growth in our climate, that within a few weeks only after sowing abundant supplies may be in hand.

The writer cannot, however, but maintain that, though at some increase of labor in the production, no expenditure on the farm may, in the long run, pay better than an annual crop of mangolds and carrots, even if raised only in sufficient quantity to alternate with the ruta baga, and thus the food be varied; a change which the milch cow, the stall-fed ox and the sheep crave equally with man. At the present time, when foreign demand for American beef and mutton has assumed gigantic proportions, the subject of *stock feeding* presents itself with increased force.

The subject is one which concerns the Union; our prosperity cannot advance faster than our progress in agriculture, whether as planters, grain producers, stock-breeders or dairymen. When they prosper all industries participate. The railroads, the mills, the forges, the shipping, find profitable employment, all are subordinate to the farmer's industry.

The Turnip.—That turnips, singly and alone, will secure health and strength and rich milk, the writer is far from maintaining; but he does contend that, in proper proportion, in suitable condition, at proper times, mixed with corn meal, shorts, oil cake, or other rich food, they will produce valuable results. To feed roots of any kind in imprudently cold stables, or, as may sometimes be seen, in the open air in inclement weather, the roots, perhaps, partially frozen, and expect favorable results, argues, to say the least, want of reflection; and where we find people say, as we sometimes do, they "can see no good in roots," we are sure to find, on inquiry, that some of the obviously rational and necessary rules of procedure in feeding have been disregarded. The experience of such people should never be taken as safe guides; but rather let us pin our faith on the systematic and successful, who use the right means to the right end. One such practical, observing, methodic man in a neighborhood, is worth a dozen who make no progress.

The writer should here refer to the value of turnips in another view, as a vegetable manure; most valuable will they be found for plowing under after the first killing frost of autumn. Sown thickly broadcast in August or September and allowed to cover the ground, they gather from earth and air a mass of fertilizing agents which will, the succeeding spring, astonish the experimenter.

Nothing we know of is so efficient, considering the small cost of time and money. Seventy to eighty days will make the crop, and at a cost not exceeding three dollars per acre. The preparation of the soil and climatic adaptation of the locality is an important prerequisite to success, both as respects the productiveness of the crop, and its cost, for it is manifest that, however valuable and desirable may be any object we seek, the cost of obtaining it may be disproportionate to its value; such is especially the case with all products of the soil.

Time of Sowing Turnips.

In the latitude of Philadelphia farmers begin to think of sowing ruta bagas about the 1st of July, and, if everything is in readiness, complete their sowing by the middle of the month. Their process is as follows: Plow the land level, harrow crosswise and lengthwise, getting it into fine tilth, then with the plow draw shallow furrows two and one-half feet apart; in these furrows the manure is spread; it may consist of any fertilizing material within reach. Of course, decomposed matter is the best, whether it be vegetable or animal; and here, we remark, it is a good plan to prepare, in advance, a compost which will readily disintegrate when spread. Where such is not at hand, any of the approved commercial fertilizers may be resorted to, but buy only from parties of good repute. When the fertilizer, if a superphosphate (or other commercial manure at about equal cost), at the rate of five hundred pounds per acre, has been spread, it is a good practice to remove the hind teeth from an ordinary cultivator, so as to adapt it to the width of the furrow, and pass it over the fertilizer, thus incorporating it with the soil. That done, the soil, divided in forming the furrows, is returned by splitting the ridges. This process will be found to form a ridge over the fertilizer some inches higher than the level of the general surface. As that is not desirable in our climate, where heat and drouth prevail, rather than excess of moisture, as in England, from whence the practice of ridging is derived, back down the ridges until they are nearly level, which brings the seed, when sown, near the manure, so important to stimulate the young plants.

Manner of Sowing Turnips.

Everything being now ready for sowing, with an approved drill, and the writer recommends the Keeler, sow the seed, and follow with a light roller if drouth prevail. The drill should be adjusted to sow not less than three pounds of seed per acre if in rows, two and one-half feet apart,—not that so much seed is necessary, if any considerable percentage vegetates and escapes the fly, the scorching sun, and other unfavorable influences. It is probable that, if eight ounces of seed could be evenly distributed, each grain germinate, and finally produce a healthy plant, there would be a sufficient number of plants to the acre; but it would be a very unwise procedure to stint the seed to save, for the present moment only, the pocket. The English, to whom we look for instruction in root culture, use seven to eight pounds per acre, but the turnip has been so generally grown in their country for generations, that the fly, fed and pampered, has become a most formidable pest; so much so that great difficulty is sometimes found in securing a "stand."

The Turnip Fly.—The "turnip fly" just referred to is a jumping beetle, of greenish-black color, and about the tenth of an inch in length, sometimes so destructive as to devour every plant before the farmer is aware that the seed has sprouted. This active little insect hibernates in protected places, and from early spring to autumn produces a rapid succession of generations. The mature insects apparently reveling upon the marrow-like material of the cotyledons and first two or three pairs of leaves of the turnip and other cruciferous plants, deposit eggs upon the leaves, which, in a few days, suffer as much from the attack of the unseen larvæ as from the parent.

The remedies, which are only palliative, are thick seeding, dashing with sulphur or plaster, light applications of carbolic or whale oil soap, etc., and when all have failed or about to fail, re-sowing in fresh ground. A wet season is prejudicial to the rapid growth of the fly, and, with a rich soil, the young plants soon acquire the third pair of leaves, which, with those succeeding, are proof against further injury.

If the sowing just described should, by the ravages of the fly or other accident, have failed, pass along the ridges with a spike-tooth harrow, to destroy any weeds which may have sprouted, and re-sow, as before. If, from the time lost, it may be deemed too late to perfect a crop of ruta bagas with certainty, it may be better to make the re-sowing with round or flat turnips, which mature in a shorter season. Supposing the sowing a success, allow the plants to reach the rough, or second leaf, then proceed thus: Taking a light steel hoe in hand, and standing so as to bring a corner of the hoe in an oblique direction with respect to the line of plants, and near to them, the operator walks backward, drawing the hoe gently, and lightly skimming the surface of the soil, and with it all young weeds which may have sprung up contemporary with the crop; returning, the opposite side of the row, or drill, is taken, thus leaving only a narrow line of turnip plants, nearly free from weeds.

Thinning Out.—After a few days, when they have grown somewhat stronger, and are too rank for the fly to injure seriously, they may be "clumped," which is performed by taking a sharp, light, steel hoe of suitable size, say three inches wide, and, standing facing the row, cut crosswise, so as to leave clumps of plants at intervals of five inches. At first the operator will cut timidly, fearing to destroy too many; but in a little while he will have gained courage, and proceed with increasing speed. It is surprising with what celerity such work may be performed by an expert, which any one may become with an hour's practice. When the plants left in clumps have fully recovered from the disturbance, which is unavoidable, and again stand erect, the process of "singling" commences; this is simply pulling out with the finger and thumb and casting aside all but the most promising plant in each group or clump. After the lapse of a few days, when the selected plants have become upright and self-sustaining, a very shallow furrow may be cast from each side, the earth thus removed meeting in a ridge between the rows. If the weather is damp they may stand thus a few days, each day adding greatly to their strength; but if the weather be hot and dry, it is better to proceed at once with the hoeing, which done, the ridge of earth is to be leveled down by a spike-tooth harrow, or, in its absence, a cultivator with well-worn teeth, taking care not to cast the earth upon the young plants. This process of plowing from the plants, and cultivating immediately after to return the soil, will need to be repeated several times during the season of growth; indeed, it may be practiced with great advantage, so long as the space between the rows is not obstructed by foliage, on each repetition inserting the plow deeper than before. Thus the crop will at length stand daily increasing in vigor and bulk, until the time arrives for placing it in winter quarters, in the latitude of Philadelphia not later than the 20th of November.

METHOD OF SAVING FOR WINTER FEEDING.

The English, who are our instructors in this branch of husbandry, and have taught us most of what we know on the subject, have some advantage in climate over Pennsylvania, though not over the South, which admits of feeding the bulbs as they stand in the ground, as well as under cover, the stock, especially sheep, being grazed upon them, using hurdles to confine the flock to a limited space. A flock destined for the butcher are first turned in, where they may feed upon the better portion, then moved into a fresh inclosure, thus exciting the appetite. These are succeeded by a store flock, which picks up the fragments, so that nothing is lost. This process corresponds with that of some of our prairie farmers, who turn their beef cattle into the standing corn (a bad practice on the Atlantic coast), and follow by hogs, which find every half digested grain passed through the cattle, and fatten sooner than on dry corn.

In America, where a five-acre patch of ruta bagas cannot be found within some of the counties, to say nothing of States, the statement may excite surprise that a hundred acres in that root on the lands of a single farmer of Great Britain is by no means unusual; and recently the writer entertained an English farmer and stock-breeder, making a tour in this country, who, himself, cultivated two hundred and fifty acres in roots annually.

Harvesting Turnips.

Of course, such large breadths demand every mechanical device and appliance for saving the crop, and instead of, as with us, each root destined to be stored being pulled up singly by the hand and cast into a heap, then again taken in hand and topped, again cast into a heap preparatory to being hauled away, they, on the contrary, top with a hoe. A light, sharp steel hoe is held perpendicularly in hand, and, with a quick action, drawn horizontally, thus decapitating each root in succession as it stands in the ground. This done, they are drawn out and into windrows by a chain-harrow. It can be readily seen with what celerity this labor may be performed, and the great saving in cost. With our small patches we can get along, however, by the old time-honored practice; with increasing breadths of land in roots will come improved methods. Some growers have already adopted new systems; instead of topping all the roots of the crop, they haul a portion, just as pulled up, top and root, to a convenient position near the stables, place them in a narrow, ridge-like form, and cover with straw, corn-fodder, or any light, trashy material which may be at hand. Thus they are preserved until New Year, or longer, using from one end, and covering up after each removal. The writer has pursued this plan for many years. It is true, in warm, damp weather, the tops partially decay, and become somewhat slimy, but the roots do not take harm, and cattle feed on them, and the tops, also, with much avidity. Perhaps a little salt sprinkled on each mess would be an advantage. For milch cows it is recommended to give salt when feeding turnips, and the better time is immediately after milking.

Pitting Turnips.—The main winter and spring stock of roots are preserved in pits, not mounds, as made in some localities, narrow pits, after this fashion: Select a suitable spot, near the stables if practicable, but surely where the drainage is good, an indispensable prerequisite; dig a trench sixteen inches wide, and as many or more inches in depth, the length as convenient or necessary. In this deposit the topped roots, and cover with the earth dug out of the trench, using a little more in addition as winter approaches. If cold may be expected in severity, place over all long stable manure, or anything which will impede the entry of frost without creating warmth. Thus the writer has found roots of all descriptions—ruta bagas, common turnips, carrots, beets, parsnips—to keep well. They are accessible at all times, and may be removed in larger or smaller quantity, as needed or desired. Altogether, it is better than mounds, which, being elevated, are exposed to frost, and require care in construction. In the pits described the writer annually keeps beets and carrots far into the spring, indeed, he has fed working oxen with beets, to their great delight, up to July 1st.

From what has been said, it may be seen that theory and practice should go hand in hand; the writer is simply describing his own operations at Bloomsdale, not telling what may possibly be done, and satisfied with the utility of his practice, confidently recommends it to others.

On the Varieties of Turnips.

In England turnips are divided into two distinct classes, those designed for stock feeding, and those for table use. They are also divided into rough-leaved and smooth-leaved. The smooth-leaved embrace those of which the ruta baga, or "Swede," is the type, and of which the purple-topped, yellow-fleshed variety may be taken as the best representative. The rough-leaved sorts are generally white-skinned and white-fleshed, some purely white, others with green or purple crowns; though there are also several rough-leaved varieties with yellow flesh. These rough-leaved sorts are again subdivided into cattle and table turnips; in the usually limited culture in this country such distinction is of little consequence. The leading varieties for cattle feeding are here described in the order of their maturity.

Large Early Red-Top Globe.—A variety of white turnip of comparatively recent introduction, of large size, and rapid growth, unusually attractive, approved and admired by all. It is recommended mainly as a valuable acquisition for feeding cattle.

Pomeranian White Globe.—This is a free growing rough-leaved sort, useful for both table and stock, and may be highly commended for both purposes. Turnip cultivators need not hesitate to sow it, whether for stock, market or family use; it is not quite so rapid in growth as the flat varieties, may be expected to come in as a succession in autumn, and is admirable for table use in early winter. In short, the "Pomeranian Globe" is eminently valuable, and supplies every want of a white-skinned variety. This is used by stock-breeders for early feeding, also for sowing at seasons too late to secure a crop of ruta bagas. It is productive, hardy, and eclipses the "White Stone."

White Norfolk Globe.—A very desirable variety, rapid in growth, globular in form, large, and an admirable keeper, recommended especially for stock feeding.

Amber Globe.—Is an Americanized foreign turnip, almost indispensable on every farm. The flesh, when the turnip is growing, has a very slight tinge of yellow, which becomes darker as the root matures; it is as solid as a ruta baga, and, if topped very closely, so as to effectually arrest sprouting, it may be kept until late in spring as good as when first gathered. The flavor is milder than that of the ruta baga, therefore by some highly esteemed for table purposes. On the whole, this is the best type of the yellow, rough-leaved sorts, and fills every want in that direction. The foliage of this variety is strap-leaved.

Yellow Aberdeen, or Yellow Scotch.—It is a highly approved cattle turnip, attains a large size, is solid, nutritious, a good keeper, and is, in every respect, reliable. There are several types under distinctive names, without much variation in quality. Full justice to this variety has not been done. Observations and experiments with the Aberdeen, raised from seed produced from American bulbs, clearly shows that it is a variety of highest merit. It is well-adapted to cattle-feeding, and for table use also, late in winter and far into the spring, when the earlier ripening varieties have grown pithy.

A friend exhibited, at mid-winter, a sample of butter made by him, which he assured us was the result of Aberdeen turnips and corn fodder only, no grain or oil food whatever having been fed. The butter was of a deep lemon tint, sweet, well-flavored, and would have commanded, at that time, eighty to ninety cents per pound in the Philadelphia market; we must not, however, fail to add, his stock was the Guernsey. His method was to feed the roots, well salted, immediately after milking, as many as each animal felt disposed to eat. Thus treated, there was no turnip flavor perceptible, either in the milk or butter.

The Swede, or ruta baga is, perhaps, the most important root cultivated for stock food; its rapid maturity, large bulk to a given area, nutritious quality and sanitary properties commend it as eminently worthy of culture. It has become a practice, in the sale of ruta baga seed, to create varieties; some actual, some fictitious, but it is best not to be misled by new names.

The Bloomsdale Swede is the result of long years of patient, critical selection, and, on comparison carefully made with intent to determine and secure the best, it was proved to be unquestionably the most desirable. The foliage is not super-abundant (as in the imported), the shape is nearly globular, the crown deep purple, the flesh a rich yellow.

BEETS FOR CATTLE.

Under this head American farmers embrace all beets with certain characteristics, whether they be for stock-feeding or sugar-making. What principally interests at present is the question, which is best for stock food; as preliminary to further remarks on beet culture, the first question to be solved by every farmer is as to his command of necessary force to accomplish, with reasonable prospect of success, what he may desire, and whether he can devote a full season's attention to the crop, or can more profitably use the time in other directions, relying on a crop of ruta baga and other turnips for succulent food, which, though not as nutritious, may be raised at less cost of time and labor.

It is emphatically with root culture as it is in all other operations on the farm, a simple question of dollars and cents, and if food less nutritious may be obtained in quantity to compensate for deficiency in quality, the inferior may be preferable. Ruta bagas, judged by that rule, may be most profitable. Each one must decide the question for himself. Where circumstances admit there need be no doubt, the greater advantage will be found in possessing both, as affording variations of diet.

Varieties of the Beet.

Long Blood Red.—This is a valuable winter table beet, and has been brought to its present state of perfection by successive yearly selections. It is preferable to the Rochester, or Radish beet, which grows above the surface and is liable to be fibrous. It is held to be as rich in saccharine as either the sugar or the mangels, with the further highly important advantage from its habit of growth, which all who, as husbandmen study our climate, can readily perceive, namely, of withstanding drouth. In our climate excessive heat, accompanied by prolonged drouth, is a usual accompaniment of our summers, and all who have cultivated either the mangels or sugar beets have observed the entire suspension of growth at such periods, the foliage drooping, frequently falling entirely, and followed by an elongated crown or a growth of woody, or, at least, fibrous matter. This substance is of little, if any, value; rejected by the stock, it simply goes to make manure. On the contrary, the long blood beet grows mainly beneath the surface, and is, on that account, less exposed to heat, and enabled to resist drouth. The writer has never failed to secure a satisfactory crop, even under adverse circumstances, ten to twelve tons can be grown to the acre—besides, the Long Blood is unquestionably very rich—the percentage of sucrose being as great as in the White Sugar.

Silesian Sugar Beet.—This is the old, well-known form of sugar beet, long raised in this country for feeding, and is one of the varieties cultivated abroad for sugar. Heretofore the great effort has been to obtain the largest bulk of root food from a given area, and where a primary object is to supply merely succulent food as distinct from dry, there is great gain in quantity. Recent chemical analysis has demonstrated that the percentage of saccharine in the large roots falls below that of the smaller, and, where the primary object is sugar, cultivators no longer aim at large roots, but rather those of medium size, well matured; hence, it follows that in feeding for flesh or for butter, the smaller roots, in proportion to the weight fed, will accomplish greater results. The beet owes its fattening influences principally to the saccharine matter contained in it. This varies according to variety, manure, soil and climatic influences. The production in Germany averages one ton of sugar to each eleven or twelve tons of roots. When fed to animals, the entire proportion of sugar is realized, and produces wonderful results.

Imperial Sugar Beet.—This, it is claimed, is the most profitable of the sugar varieties, being richer in saccharine qualities than the preceding. It has a smooth skin, and shows the results of careful selection and breeding.

MANGEL WURZEL.

There are several sub-varieties of the Long Mangel, known as the Mammoth Long Red, Long Yellow, Long Oxhorn, Long White Green Topped; but the writer will here confine his remarks to the first, inasmuch as it embraces all the good qualities of others, and there can be no advantage in dividing attention between it and other sorts of similar shape and properties. The one referred to has long been cultivated as the mangel wurzel *par excellence.* In England, eighty tons have frequently grown to the acre; in this country, thirty tons may be considered a good crop.

Red and Yellow Globe.—There are two round types of mangels, each possessing very similar qualities; indeed, the distinction is mainly in color, and, hence, simply a matter of fancy in the cultivator. For facility of harvesting the crop the globe form has an advantage over the long, as is evident at sight; and a further, and, possibly, more important advantage, is the smaller waste in fibrous neck, and there is less liability to suffer, in extreme drouth, an important consideration, in our climate. Seventy tons to the acre is not uncommon in England.

Yellow Oval, or Intermediate.—This variety, having much to commend it, commands a large share of favor. It is a productive variety, raised with great success on any good soil.

Golden Tankard.—A heavy producer. The richest colored and smoothest skinned of the family of mangels, and the most nutritious in its albuminous compounds, proving forty per cent. higher than the long red mangel. The roots of this variety are perfect pictures. It is distinct in every particular, even to the color of the leaves, the ribs and leaf stems being quite golden.

CULTIVATION.

The soil selected should be a light loam, free from hard clay, and if of a slightly calcareous nature, so much the better; plow deeply, when the apple is in blossom, as a guide to the season; later the crop may be overtaken by drouth. Harrow thoroughly, furrow out to a depth of eight inches with a double mold board plow, if such can be had, or, if not, with an ordinary plow, casting the earth both ways. Apply in the furrow a liberal dressing of well-rotted stable manure, or about twenty dollars' worth per acre of commercial fertilizer, the component parts of which should be soluble phosphate of lime, potash, nitrogen and sulphate of lime. After the application of the fertilizer run a subsoil plow in the open furrows, breaking up the hard pan and distributing the manure. Deep culture is a necessity to success, and the sub-soil plow the most important implement, as every inch the soil is deepened permits the roots to draw nutriment from an additional hundred tons of earth per acre. Next, split the ridges covering the fertilizer, and, transposing the relative positions of ridge and furrow, back down the new ridges nearly to the level of the field, and drill upon the flat so formed, the seed thus being placed directly over the fertilizer and broken subsoil. If the weather be dry, a roller should follow the seed drill, to insure germination. An advantage will be found in preparing the ground, applying the fertilizer and splitting the ridges, a fortnight in advance of drilling, that a portion of the fertilizer may have assumed an assimilable form for the early subsistence of the young plants. A light dressing of common salt applied to the soil will be found beneficial to the best crop, especially in dry soil. When the young plants are half an inch high, they should be side-scraped with steel hoes, and then cross-cut with four-inch hoes into clumps of three or four plants, the clumps to be afterwards reduced to one plant by hand-weeding as more fully described under the head of Turnips. This process will give about thirty thousand plants to the acre if the stand be good.

The crop should be kept free from weeds, and the soil loose, that air and moisture may more freely penetrate to the roots. With thorough cultivation and subsoil breaking in mid-summer, the roots are not so liable to suffer from variations of temperature and moisture; hence, the growth is more uniform, and the roots are less weedy and distorted. During the entire culture care must be taken not to injure the leaves of the plants, as with impaired lungs, a healthy action is impossible.

When the roots are fully developed, and ripe, which will be about the first of October (and may be known by the stoppage of circulation), they should be taken up; if they make a second growth, under certain atmospheric influences, a large portion of the saccharine matter goes to form new leaves. On the other hand, they should not be disturbed before maturity, as the formation of saccharine matter is most rapid at that period. The roots can be taken out by passing a subsoil plow under them, which, if run deep enough, will escape all but the extreme points, and the saving in time more than compensates for the loss of product.

Care must be taken in harvesting the roots, that they be not bruised; those thus injured are apt to decay. The tops should be cut so closely as to remove all leaf-buds, as the dampness of the pits may cause the embryo buds to burst forth, and thus exhaust nutritious qualities. The roots, when pulled, should be pitted without delay, as described for ruta bagas or "Swedes." The European growers of beets have a proverb, "Out of the earth into the earth," and with care they may be kept till the first of July.

And here, to avoid the necessity of repetition, we will say that the foregoing remarks apply equally as well to the culture of the carrot and parsnip. Every stock breeder should grow the beet, in some of its varieties, as he may lay up for winter a valuable supply of this food at times when Swedes or turnips have failed, by reason of the fly or dry weather. The beet, though requiring earlier planting, is for that reason more reliable in vegetating, and is well established before the blazing days of July, when the turnips are just breaking ground, perhaps to be devoured by the fly. The beet leaves may flag at midday, but next morning the cells are distended, the leaves crisp and full of vigor. Extensive breadths of sugar beets are grown in Southern

Europe, where the Swede is seldom seen, at least, never raised for cattle, because of the hot sun and dry soils. The beet, for feeding market cattle, is unsurpassed, and, by deep pitting, can be kept from season to season. By the practice of deep pitting the writer was enabled, at the International Centennial Exhibition, May 15th to June 1st, to exhibit twenty varieties of beets, one bushel of each, preserved in perfect condition, as sweet and crisp as when taken from the field in November, also carrots in equally good condition. Southern readers are advised to try the beet, believing that they will realize a profit.

ESTIMATE OF COST.

A crop of ten tons of beets can be produced at an expenditure varying from thirty to forty dollars. The following estimate may be taken as an approximation, soil, situation, cost of labor and fertilizers, all having, however, an important bearing upon the cost:

Rent of land	$ 7.00
Plowing, harrowing and rolling	3.50
Ridging, application of manure and subsoiling	3.00
Manure	18.00
Drilling	.50
Thinning, weeding and hoeing	4.00
Three cultivations	3.00
Two hoeings	5.00
Subsoiling between rows	2.00
Lifting the crop	3.00
Total	$49.00

The ten tons, under this estimate, would cost less than five dollars a ton, or about twelve cents a bushel, and in the cultivation of large breadths the cost per acre can be reduced, while the production may be increased twenty-five to fifty per cent.

THE CARROT.

To the dairyman whose object is gilt-edged butter during winter, commanding readily double the price of the ordinary market grade, carrots may be considered indispensable. They not only give the richness of sweet vernal grass to the milk and cream, but color the butter naturally, beside which all artificial methods are imperfect and unsatisfactory. To the country family, which can afford the higher comforts of life, and with whom butter is not simply something so-called, irrespective of quality, perhaps lard-like in substance, flavor and color, the carrot need not be commended; it speaks its own praise.

To the dairyman, whose object is simply milk, and milk only, the ruta baga and the beet may supply his wants; they can be, especially the former, produced at less cost than the carrot, and will yield as great, or even greater, flow of milk, an advantage which need not be enlarged upon, and it is certain where either is fed in connection with only a moderate addition of farinaceous food, as Indian meal, in preference to all else, butter of prime quality may be obtained.

The Varieties. Orange Danvers, Half Long.—A valuable sort of the Half Long type, admirable in color, fixed in habit, a wonderful producer, the best of all for the stock breeder, and valuable to the market gardener. With this variety the planter secures the largest return to the acre with the least difficulty of harvesting.

Long Orange, or Long Red Surrey.—The Long Orange carrot is an old standby for winter use. Raise more than needed for table use and share with the cow, she will make ample return for the kindness, filling the pail with rich milk, and giving the butter the color and flavor of that from grass.

Long White Belgian and Large Yellow Belgian.—These vary, principally in color, and produce a larger return than other Carrots. To the milkman and to the stock-feeder they are worth much more than the cost of culture, promote liberal secretion of milk of improved quality over that from dry food, and may be fed alternately with ruta bagas and beets, with the best results. The stock-feeder will find them of high value. Fed to the stalled ox, or the wether, being fattened for the butcher, or the ewe strengthened to nourish the early lamb, succulent food, just such as the carrot gives, is indispensable. The experienced feeder will be cautious lest he overdo the thing, and on the first evidence of failing appreciation of the special food supplied, will substitute some other; hence, the importance of providing variety; and just here comes in the opportunity to recommend a portion of each, ruta bagas, beets and carrots, so as to alternate as needed, each heavily dusted with Indian meal and bran, and a proper portion of salt, the roots, of course, previously prepared by washing and slicing.

CULTIVATION.

The field culture of the carrot is identical with that prescribed for the beet, in every particular; the processes are the same, and the time of sowing, also. Crops of eighteen hundred bushels have been raised to the acre, and one-third of that quantity may be confidently looked for under proper conditions of soil, culture and season.

Cultivators are advised to run a subsoil breaker upon both sides of each row at least twice during the season of growth, especially if drouth prevails, that the fibers may be better enabled to extend, and for the promotion of subterranean circulation. This process is recommended for the culture of the beet and mangel. The cost, per acre, of producing a crop of carrots (allowing twenty dollars for manure, and twenty dollars for preparation and culture) should not exceed forty dollars; which, at four hundred bushels, would be ten cents a bushel, and at six hundred bushels, less than seven cents per bushel, for a crop, the profits and advantages of which need not be enlarged upon.

PRESERVATION OF CARROTS.

The carrot does not keep well, except in cool weather, and even in winter more care is requisite than with either the ruta baga or beet. It is, therefore, well to so adjust the consumption of the crop, that it be used up in season. The narrow trench method of storing beets for winter use, is emphatically the one for this root, above all others; do not trust them in a cellar, even, though it be cool, nor in mounds piled two or three feet high, as was, and is still, practiced.

The methodical farmer will not be alarmed at the injunction of caution; he knows it is better not to attempt anything which cannot be done well, and, having once commenced a job, the only economic course is to see it effectually finished.

KOHL RABI, OR TURNIP-ROOTED CABBAGE.

This plant is a variation of the cabbage family, fixed in character by long years of selection. The stem above ground grows into globular, or olive-shaped form, and possesses features common to both cabbage and turnips. It is used both for table use and stock feeding, and in parts of England, where turnips can no longer be produced, it has widely taken their place, yielding from twenty-five to thirty-five tons to the acre. Only a few localities are suitable to its growth, the requisites being a moist atmosphere and soil. In this country success can only be assured on the seacoast or on damp lowlands.

The seed, two pounds to the acre, should be sown five to six weeks earlier than Swedes or ruta bagas. The land should be furrowed out at two and one-half feet, and dressed with an ammoniacal fertilizer, dried fish, marl or guano, the furrows closed and the seed drilled on top after smoothing down. The young plants should be cut out to ten inches apart. The plant is quite hardy, the roots resisting the effects of frost for a long time; very useful for sheep feeding in winter. There are three leading sorts, viz.:

Purple.—A variety having a blue purple skin.

White Vienna.—Very choice—smooth light green skin. Very few and very small leaves.

Large Green.—Large bulb, green skinned. Leafy.

THE PARSNIP.

The original of the cultivated parsnip is found growing wild in England, the root white, aromatic, mucilaginous, sweet, and possessing a degree of acridity which it loses by cultivation.

In our experiments in search of facts to be used for our own advantage in stock feeding, and to be communicated for public good, we have, from time to time, raised the parsnip for the purpose of feeding to a herd of Channel Island cattle, but the results have not convinced us of the economy, in comparison with other roots, for horned cattle. There is this advantage, however; the parsnip never rots when stored, and if work presses, may be left out over winter so far north as Philadelphia without loss, thus reserving this special crop for spring feeding.

Bloomsdale.—A selection from the Hollow Crowned, shorter, thicker, easier to take all out of the ground, and producing more tons to the acre.

Sugar, or Cup.—An old variety, longer and slimmer than the Bloomsdale, the variety usually sold. It is said that the excellence claimed for Guernsey hams is attributable to the parsnip, which is a prominent food for the hog of that island; it may be well for some one among ourselves, who has the opportunity, to test the fact. In sections where frost does not interfere, a portion of the crop may be left over winter and the hogs fed upon them as they stand, the proportion of saccharine matter being increased by frost, and the roots rendered still more palatable. It seems practicable, by this method, for breeders of swine to accomplish, in the Southern States, results highly profitable, in comparison with cost of culture.

The writer desires, with this in view, to urge the culture of parsnips in all swine-breeding sections, the cost of the crop being simply the culture and manure, while production can be made to reach ten tons of roots, possessing nine per cent. of sugar.

Time of Sowing Parsnips.—The seed of the parsnip, though vegetating freely under favorable conditions, not infrequently fails when sown late, when heat and drouth prevail; hence, it should precede the carrot and the beet by some days; a good guide to time of sowing being the blooming of the cherry. The directions for the culture of the beet apply to the parsnip.

In conclusion, the writer will observe that the culture of roots entails trouble and expense, and that no one should attempt it unless determined to succeed. Farming is, with Americans, in by far too many cases, a slipshod business. The merchant, the manufacturer, the master-mechanic, who should conduct his affairs with careless irregularity, indifferent to cost as compared with compensation, who should be found unprepared at the moment of pressing demands upon him, surely could not expect a successful issue to his efforts; and why should the tiller of the soil expect exemption from results almost inevitable? Farmers, as a class, are laborious enough—in many cases, far too plodding; thought and reflection, united with physical exertion, would accomplish more. A fruitful source of disappointment proceeds from our attempting too much in proportion to our means; not infrequently, larger breadths of land are designed for crops than the capital at command warrants. With the farmer, capital means laborers, manure, working stock and numerous incidentals, and the land marked out for cropping should ever be subordinate to these. In tillage it is, by far, better to do a little well; there may be profit in that; the reverse is certain to result in loss.

CHAPTER XXII.

Packing and Shipping Vegetables.

As a rule all the products of the garden, not grown on trees and hardwooded vines, are usually called vegetables, but at least one-half are really fruits. A bean, pea, tomato, eggplant, melon and squash, is as much a fruit as an apple or peach, for their enlargement is subsequent to flowering. They are borne on the flower stems and are the results of fertilized flowers. That kind of garden plant alone is a culinary vegetable which develops tissue under ground, as in the turnip, carrot, onion, parsnip; or above ground as in the leaf-stalks of celery, or leaves of the cabbage, lettuce and parsley. All these growths are independent of sexual results, and as a rule these plants require cooking to prepare them for food, although there are a few exceptions.

These distinctions, however, do not bring cash to the market gardener. He must, after growing the articles, look for his profit in good packing, quick transportations, honest commission agents and a judicious selection of markets.

The prices obtained by southern market gardeners shipping truck to Philadelphia, New York and other distant points, depends so much upon the manner of packing that it is a subject to which too much attention cannot be given.

To illustrate: Florida egg plants sent to Philadelphia about May 1st command $7.00 per barrel-crate, but later on in the season, as the temperature increases, they arrive, often due to bad packing and slow transportation, in such decayed condition as to be worthless. Cucumbers, in the Philadelphia market about the last of May, are usually worth $1.00 per dozen, but as the warmer weather of June approaches many arrive in such bad condition as often to remain unsold. Beans in this market command in April about $5.00 per crate, but in May are often unsalable on account of bad packing, insufficient ventilation in cars and the holds of steamships. Such perishable articles should be shipped only in crates holding not over one bushel, better one-half bushel, as beans and peas when discolored are unsalable. Forty-eight hours in early spring is as long as peas will safely carry, sometimes one day is more than they will stand.

Tomatoes sent to Philadelphia from the far South in March and April are worth $3.00 to $5.00, but are so likely to decay during the warm weather of June as to be unprofitable, or perhaps because they come into competition with the new crop from Maryland and Delaware. Tomato crates should not be over one-half bushel in capacity, and the fruit when picked not be over half ripe. Two days' carriage is as much as they will withstand.

Ventilated Packages.—It cannot be doubted that the shipping season for vegetables could be much prolonged by the use of better packages and better freight cars, the sound condition being prolonged in proportion as the packages are well ventilated, and, on the other hand, the rotted condition increased in the proportion of non-ventilation.

All vegetables and fruits generate heat and moisture, and to an increasing extent as the temperature rises. A rapid removal of these exhalations, as they are in the open air while the fruit or vegetable remains growing, preserves them in good condition, but to keep the vegetables in a close, confined atmosphere hastens fermentation and decay. The packages should be small, as bulk is a hindrance to ventilation. Barrels are bad packages; better use double sized flat crates, with a partition. Costly refrigeration is not necessary if thorough ventilation can be obtained, and it cannot be doubted that ice cold refrigeration ruins the flavor of fruits and vegetables. Also fruits of hard-wooded plants, as peaches, grapes and pears, and, we may add, strawberries, require more careful handling than vegetables, but no fruit will require more careful treatment, critical sorting and packing than tomatoes, egg-plants and cucumbers. These the trucker should pick when of full size, and just as the ripening process is about to set in, which condition is indicated by a distention of the tissues and a disposition to change color. No trucker who expects to make a reputation should ship small or defective stock; in fact he should put himself in the place of a city purchaser, and consider what he would buy from a green grocer or provision dealer, and ship only such quality.

Crates and Packages.—When packing vegetables or fruit for market, do not use close boxes, or even ordinary slatted boxes. Well-made ventilated fruit and vegetable packages can be purchased in every section of the country where market gardening is pursued. Of course, some forms of packages are better than others. Light packages save freight and insure more careful handling.

Sorting for Packing.—The sorting of vegetables or fruits for shipment demands so much care that every imperfect specimen should be rejected. The packing should not be done under a broiling sun, but under a shed or tree, so that the goods may be cooled off by every passing breeze, for, if packed in temperature of 90° or

100°, they will, when put into close cars, soon develop a temperature 20° or 30° higher consequent upon a fermentation which might otherwise be avoided, or certainly deferred.

Pack snugly, using just enough force to place them sufficiently tight to prevent shifting. Avoid baskets, as top weight injures specimens at bottom. See to it particularly that every package contains uniform specimens. Do not mix culls or second grade stock with first class, for by so doing the contents of a full package is rated at the market value of the lower grade which it contains.

Outwardly, packages should be neat and attractive, as first appearances influence values. Every thoughtful shipper of vegetables or fruits is not only led to pack uniformly throughout his crates, but to ship in crates bearing his name, so that what reputation he makes for himself may benefit him through dealers knowing his name and address. Oranges and vegetables from certain parties in Florida have brought much better prices and met with quicker sales than equally good products from other parties, simply because the brand on the package was a positive guarantee of quality.

The market is seldom broken in prices by good fruits or vegetables; it is the misshapen, unripe and badly selected products which injure the sale of a better article. The inexperienced grower of vegetables or fruits does not have a conception of how the crates are handled before reaching the possession of the retail dealer. Depot porters, freight handlers, expressmen, draymen, storekeepers, all working in a hurry and doing their share to shake up and crush the contents, if not to break the package. It may be safely estimated that an ordinary crop is handled fourteen or fifteen times before reaching the consumer.

The shipper must not imagine that *his* goods are to receive special attention from transportation companies or from commission men. The companies care little for his individual interest, and the commission men, if doing a business of any volume, have no time to look to special cases, but endeavor to deal equally with all who look to them as agents.

Early Shipments.—Early shipments are always profitable when the fruit or vegetable is properly developed, but quality should be aimed at by the grower, rather than early, large, or extensive shipments. As an example of the evil effects to produce quantity at the expense of quality, notice the result of the introduction of the Kolb Gem watermelon, an early, reliable sort, a good shipper, showy outwardly, but in quality only third class, so poor in texture and flavor that the consumption of early watermelons by people of discrimination has fallen off to over one-half, because it is impossible to obtain anything but a miserable Kolb Gem until Northern grown watermelons come into the market.

Quality Most Important.—Quality should never be sacrificed to quantity, either in the production of enormous yields to the acre or in the production of monstrous specimens, as so often is the case in cabbage and cucumbers.

Market Quotations.—Truckers to be successful salesmen should be subscribers to one or more of Produce Journals, that they may familiarize themselves with the wants and conditions of the various markets, sending their products where they are most likely to bring the best prices. Supplies and prices, however, vary in nothing so much as in fruits and vegetables. Cities like Philadelphia, New York, or Boston, may take at a good price a thousand crates of cucumbers in one day, and the next day decline them at any price.

Freight Cars.—However cautious the shipper may be, his care and labor is defeated if the railway companies do not furnish freight cars of such design as to keep a steady stream of outside air passing through and over the load, thereby insuring good ventilation. It would seem that it is the railway companies which are responsible for dumping upon us, in the months of May and June, such quantities of half diseased green fruit and vegetables.

The grower of garden vegetables for shipment should plant a variety and not confine himself to one, as cucumbers, cabbage or tomatoes, for he never knows when the market will be glutted, and if it be of that sort on which he has built his expectations of profit he may be sadly disappointed. In shipping, it is better to ship continuously to three or four established markets than to attempt to follow high quotations from various sources, as the conditions which regulate the prices may change daily, and points offering highest prices one day may be lowest the next.

It is a mistake to divide a limited quantity of fruit or vegetables between many commission merchants, as the returns in small consignments are eaten up by the expenses of cartage and handling.

CHAPTER XXIII.

Implements for the Farm and Garden.

The improvements in the design and practicability of farming and gardening implements and tools, during the last fifty years, has fully kept pace with the mechanical development in machinery used in other arts, and it may not be out of place to make a brief reference to the leading mechanical contrivances used for vegetable gardening.

Plows.—The prices for the ordinary wood or iron beam plows range from five to twenty dollars, and for the sulky plows, on which the plowman rides, from forty-five to sixty dollars. In these different makes are variations in the arrangement of the handles and beams, but the principal difference consists in the length, angle, twist or curve of the mould-board, the adjustment of the share or point, and the ease of draft. It sometimes happens that the plow most popular or which seems to be adapted to one particular section does not have the same reputation in another.

This sometimes arises in a great measure from local fancy or prejudice, sometimes from different conditions of soil.

A good plow is a necessity to good farming, and the farmer will do best to select one that has proved to be adapted to his locality and is known to his plowmen.

Hillside Plows.—Besides the ordinary farm or level land plow, is the hillside or swivel plow, arranged to have the mould-board and point swing on either side of the beam, so that the furrow slice may be turned down hill and all the furrows lap in one direction, to prevent washing. This form of plow is sometimes used for level land plowing, as it leaves the field without a center or dead furrow, and for that reason the small sizes are often preferred by market gardeners. The sizes made are adapted to one, two, three or four horses, and prices range from five to twenty-five dollars.

Subsoil Plows.—These are used to follow the furrow made by the surface plows. The object of the subsoil plowing is to open and loosen the strata beneath the furrow of the ordinary plow, that the soil may be deepened, drained, and consequently made warmer. As a rule it is desirable to simply open the soil, as stirring up and mixing the upper and lower strata generally proves injurious, except when done with great caution. The depth of opening attained by subsoil plows varies from fifteen to twenty inches. Sizes are made to suit one to three horses. The smallest size is mostly used for garden culture.

Ridging or Double Mould-Board Plows are useful for opening furrows to receive manure, and for closing the same, forming alternate ridges upon which to drill, and for plowing or hilling up, for shallow ditching, and for listing corn.

Sod and Subsoil Plows are those in which two plows follow each other on one beam, one plowing the sod and the other the lower soil. Too heavy for ordinary use.

Cabbage Plows are small, one-horse plows, made with a low and short mould-board, so as to plow close to the row without disturbing the plants.

Potato Plows, made for plowing out potatoes, are constructed with high standards to prevent clogging, have double mould-boards, from the rear of which prongs or fingers extend, which separate the potatoes from the soil.

Potato Diggers are machines made with a wide shear or scoop in front, running under the potato hills, raising the potatoes to a large sieve or grate in the rear, from which they are carried over and deposited in convenient position to be lifted. Capacity with two horses said to be four to five acres per day.

Harrows.—The harrow is the next important implement in the preparation of the soil; the old style heavy wooden beam harrows are being superseded by the lighter iron and steel frame harrows. Many of these are arranged so that the teeth may be changed from a perpendicular to a slanting position; they then constitute what is called smoothing harrows. The wooden frame harrows are made square and double, with steel teeth.

Disk Harrows.—In addition to the harrows with teeth, others are made with revolving disks. In tearing old unbroken sod, hard baked or crusted land, black bottom land, the disk harrow requires less power to operate, and produces better results. The operator rides on the machine. Seeders are sometimes attached, so that the land is prepared and seeded at one operation.

Other harrows are made with revolving steel blades or knives, cutting into the soil and pulverizing it thoroughly. The same advantages are claimed for these as for the disk harrows.

The Acme Pulverizing Harrow, Clod Crusher and Leveler, is constructed with a double row of adjustable reversible coulters, does good work and, consequently, has a wide reputation. The Spring Tooth harrow is another valuable form. The frame is the shape of a triangle; one end of each tooth is attached to the frame, the other drags on the ground, tearing up the soil and pulverizing it.

Clod Crushers are shaped like a large roller, sometimes with spike-like projectures, others being with prismatic surfaces. It is a very valuable implement for pulverizing lumpy and heavy clay soils.

The Meeker Disk Smoothing Harrow and Crusher is principally used by truckers in preparing the soil for sowing fine seeds. It consists of a frame about six feet square, having four sets of rollers. On the two forward rollers the disks are set six inches apart. On the two rear rollers the disks are set three inches apart, and work between the forward rollers. An adjustable center-board acts as a leveller.

Manure Spreaders.—These were introduced some years ago, but, in consequence of their cost and the reluctance of gardeners to abandon old methods, have not met with the success that their importance would seem to justify. The advantages of the spreading machine is the ability to do twice the amount of work as in the old way, adding much to the value of the manure by more thorough pulverization and more even distribution.

The Lime Spreader.—This is another very useful implement. There are several makes, varying slightly in details. Distributing lime is very laborious and unpleasant, and a machine that will relieve the farmer of this labor should be in more general use.

Horse Grain and Seed Drills and Fertilizing Distributers are manufactured in different localities throughout the country, on the same general principles, but varying in many particulars, as the arrangement of the tubes, rollers, feed cog gear, gauging levers, etc. Competition necessarily compels manufacturers to construct their machines with most desirable improvements. The machines are intended to sow all kinds of grain, grass seed and fertilizers, in any desired quantity or depth, and, as a rule, give general satisfaction.

Broadcast Fertilizer Distributers are another contribution to the list of labor-saving implements. They are arranged to sow commercial fertilizers, ashes, plaster, to crush lumps and hard substances, and sow damp as regularly as dry materials. They are said to be simple, practical and durable.

Hand Drills for Sowing Garden Seeds.—There are quite a number of different makers of these machines, all claiming to be the best. The principal leading machines are the Keeler, New Model, Mathews, Planet Jr., Big Comstock, Matthew Improved. With one of these little machines the gardener can open the furrows, sow the seed, cover and roll at one time. In addition to small seeds these machines can be regulated to sow corn, beans or peas on a limited scale.

Corn Planters.—On large farms, particularly in the Western States, planting corn by hand is almost entirely abandoned in favor of the more rapid and profitable mode of planting in rows with horse power. These machines are arranged to plant single or double rows. In some machines the dropper receives its motion from the wheels running over the surface of the ground, and in others the dropping is accomplished by raising a lever at the required distance, by hand or by wires. Fertilizers are also dropped in the rows by special attachments.

Hand Corn Droppers are also extensively used, and there are many patterns of these machines. One of the best is Fisk's Automatic; it weighs between four and five pounds, and is said to plant in all kinds and conditions of soil as fast as a one-horse drill.

Broadcast Seed Sowers, for sowing all kinds of grain, grass and clover seeds, are made to operate by hand or horse power. The hand machines are capable of sowing from four to six acres per hour, and the horse machines much more. The hand machines will cover a swath of from fifteen to thirty-six feet, according to weight of the seed being sown, the lighter seeds carrying the lesser and the heavy seeds the greater distance. The power machine will carry a little wider swath. They are arranged to be attached to any ordinary farm wagon. The Pearce's Improved Cahoon machine is believed to be the best, but there are several other approved machines.

The Potato Planter.—This is one of the most important additions to modern agricultural machinery. The old mode of dropping the potato cuttings, piece by piece, is a very slow and laborious operation, and on large areas is almost prohibitory. The introduction of the planters have changed all this. They are being introduced into all sections and seem to give universal satisfaction. One man with a machine and team can plant from six to eight acres per day. The machine can be set to plant from ten to twenty-six inches apart in the drills, the depth of planting being regulated by the driver. The marking out, plowing furrow, dropping potato seed, either whole or in pieces, drilling fertilizer and covering, all constitute one operation.

Rollers.—Field and garden rollers are used at all seasons when the soil is not wet, to crush clods and compress the earth, either before or after seeding, and on grass lands and grain fields in the early spring after frost is out. There is, unfortunately, very little improvement in this implement over those used fifty years ago; they are made of wood, cast iron and wrought iron, some in one section, others from two to six sections. The rollers in sections have the advantage of turning without dragging. Sizes usually made are from single sections twelve inches wide to the six section field roller seventy-two inches wide. The field rollers are supplied with a box to hold additional weight.

Cultivators or Horse Hoes.—These are used for cultivating corn, potatoes, cabbages, etc., loosening the soil and destroying weeds between the rows, also for throwing the earth to or from the plants. They are constructed with wrought iron frames, movable and adjustable teeth. By changing the plates and moving the standards, one machine can be adapted to many different purposes. These machines are manufactured by many different parties throughout the country, but the Iron Age and Planet Jr. seem to have the lead in favor.

Lee's Horse Hoe.—This is practically a weeding machine drawn by one horse, has a wooden frame shaped like a cultivator, with eight curved spike teeth in front followed by two flat hoes or knives; the front teeth loosen the surface and the flat hoes shave off the weeds, leaving them on the surface to die. Crops can be hoed with these machines long before other cultivators can be used, as they can cut within half an inch of a row without disturbing the plants.

Two-Horse Sulky Cultivators, with two wheels and a seat for the driver, and the Two-Horse Walking Cultivators are in use on many ordinary farms, but are particularly useful on large plantations. Working two rows at one operation, they accomplish twice as much as the ordinary cultivator. They are made with the reversible plate teeth, or spring teeth, and are constructed so as to be entirely under the control of the operator.

Hand Garden Hoes.

Notwithstanding the introduction of improved wheel hoes, garden cultivators and garden plows, the hand hoe still retains its position as an indispensable tool. The half-moon hoe, the square hoe and the scuffle hoe, relics of a past age, are, under modification, still in use, made of better and lighter material, and of superior design. It will suffice to notice a few.

The Warren Hoe is a heart-shaped pointed hoe, having a ridge in the center with sides slightly concave. The operator may use the point, the sides or the wing tips, to obtain advantageous positions around growing plants. These hoes cost from fifty-five to sixty-five cents.

Reversible Scuffle Hoe.—This has an A-shaped blade, the shank of which works in a curved slot, controlled by a thumb-screw; the hoe may be set at any angle, either to push or draw.

The Crescent Hoe, so named from the shape of the blade, has a sharp edge on the outer and inner circle. It is a form of scuffle hoe.

The Weed Annihilator is a hoe having two blades crossing each other, held together in the center by a screw bolt connected with the shank of the handle. It is used as a scuffle hoe, the blades being expanded or contracted as desired.

The Onion Weeder is a small triangular hoe, three inches wide on the broad end, handle about eight inches long.

The Celery Hoe has a blade fourteen inches wide and eight inches deep, made especially for hilling up celery. Handle six feet long.

The Trowel Hoe is shaped like a trowel and used for marking out or stirring the earth in very narrow spaces.

The Nurseryman's Hoe has two prongs about nine inches long. It is designed for grubbing around trees.

The Hexamer Hoe has six steel prongs, wedged into a clamp at the end of a five foot handle. It is valuable for loosening earth too hard for the ordinary hoe, and especially for working in stony gronnd. May be reduced to four or two prongs by drawing the wedge; broken tines may be replaced in the same manner.

Planet Celery Earther or Hiller. — This, a two-horse implement, is something like a cultivator, but, in place of the side arms, has two hilling steel wings forty-five inches long, the rear ends of which may be expanded or contracted to such varying widths of rows, or the wings may be elevated as the hilling becomes higher. It is also made with a single wing. An iron rod called a leaf lifter runs from end to end of the machine outside of the wings and lifts the leaves, that the earth may be thrown up close against the stems. The machine is also useful in cultivating sweet potatoes.

Wheel Hoes.

Lee's Wheel Hoe.—The invention of a market gardener, resultant from many years experience, is a simple and effective tool. It has a triangular or V shaped iron frame, with five light harrow teeth in front followed by a flat steel knife for cutting weeds. The teeth loosen the earth, and the knife cuts off the weeds beneath the surface, leaving them on the surface to die, so that the work does not have to be repeated for the same growth of weeds. The ends of the knife are flanged upwards to prevent the earth covering small plants. The handles reach down to a wheel in front, giving the operator perfect command of the machine.

The Planet, Jr.—A double and single wheel machine hoe, one form consisting of an iron frame having two wheels in front designed to straddle the row, the other form one wheel only for cultivating between rows. A number of attachments are used, designed for different modes of cultivation.

The Gem of the Garden is also operated by a single wheel or two wheels. It is a light, handy implement, having attachments of plows, hoes and scarifiers suited for the cultivation of vegetables of all kinds.

The Jewel single and double wheel hoe is very similar to the Gem, differing in the arrangement of the attachments.

The Comstock Garden Cultivator and Weeder.—A single wheel hoe of iron frame, and with steel teeth adapted to cultivating onions, beets, carrots, etc. Is a light running machine, doing good work.

The Universal Hoe, single or double wheel, has blades on each side, adjusted by springs.

The Matthew Weeder, of wooden frame, one wheel, hoes with standard and steel plates.

The Champion Weeder, iron frame, handles and wheel, with a single flat pointed steel hoe, very light and easily handled.

The Rotating Hand Cultivator and Weeder has iron frame, driving wheel and ratchet wheel. The knives are of steel.

Hand Plows, for use in the garden, are extensively used, and are very efficient in the making of plots too small for a horse plow and too large to dig by hand. Some are made with a long handle by which the operator draws the plow after him, others having a wheel in front are made to push. The hand plow may be made as useful in the garden as the ordinary plow in the field, as frequent cropping at odd times is rendered easy by hand plowing when horse plowing is impracticable.

Fumigators.—Fumigation is at times a necessity in the greenhouse or conservatory, to destroy by suffocation red spiders and some other insect pests, so difficult to reach that applications by syringes or sprayers fail to kill. Among fumigators may be named the following as efficient:

Perlich's Excelsior Fumigator, made in the form of a sheet-iron cone, small at the top and gradually widening, and covering a box with perforated top. Tobacco stems are packed in the cone and lighted charcoal placed in the fire box beneath, which draws its air from the outside, the suffocating tobacco fumes being ejected from the top. The apparatus is perfectly safe and does not require watching. They are also used in hospitals and ships in case of infectious diseases.

The Eureka Fumigator. — This resembles the Excelsior, the difference in the arrangement being very slight.

Woodaisne Fumigator Bellows. — These are very efficient for fumigating single plants or small conservatories.

Spraying Machines and Atomizers. — The increase in the depredations of insects of both old and new species consequent upon the vast extension of cultivation of vegetables, fruits and flowers, and the extension of inter-state commerce, has necessitated the invention and manufacture of numerous machines adapted for spraying and puffing insecticides, liquid and dry, for the destruction of such pests.

Some of these inventions are adapted to small operations, both in-doors and out. Others of larger capacity are intended to operate in the fields or orchards.

Beginning with the smaller instruments, there are sprinklers, sprayers and injectors, for use in the conservatory; garden and greenhouse syringes, made of brass or tin; bellows for spraying liquid, Peck's sprinkler, brass and tin portable pumps, insect powder-guns, dredgerbox powder sifter, etc.

For the more extended operations in the field, among the many machines for that purpose, a new device, copied from the French, has been introduced, which is said to give very satisfactory results. It consists of a flat copper or tin can, designed to contain liquid, and be carried on the back of the operator as a soldier carries his knapsack. The operator with one hand works a little force pump connected with the machine, and with the other hand directs a spraying hose upon the plants. In this way he is enabled to get over considerable ground in a short time and do effective work.

A popular device is that of a barrel on wheels, with a pump attached, for throwing or spraying liquid on trees and plants. Instead of a force pump, a pipe or hose is sometimes attached to the bottom of a barrel elevated on wheels.

Boxes on wheels, called garden engines, having a pump attachment, are used for spraying trees and plants.

A very simple arrangement has been in use for some years past for distributing, sprinkling or dusting Paris green and other powders on two rows of plants at one operation. It consists of a barrow, with a single wheel operating two revolving perforated cylinders, one on each side of the barrow, and from which the powder is sifted on the plants.

The Farmer's Favorite Distributer consists of a tin cylinder with perforated bottom, carried in the hand like a bucket, with which the operator dusts the plants as he walks along.

Grass Edgers.—On all well managed lawns the edges of walks and roads are kept free from straggling grass by several devices. For small lawns the edging knife is all-sufficient; it is a crescent-shaped steel blade, with a handle socket in which may be placed a long or short handle.

The Lightning Lawn Edge-Trimmer.—This has a revolving steel disc, fastened to the edge of a long handle. Pushed by the operator the disc is put into rapid motion. A simple and efficient tool.

Grass-Edging Shears, although old in style are

still in use. They have two handles about three feet long; the blades work vertically, resting on a small wheel.

The Planet Jr. Grass Edger is operated by two handles attached to an iron frame, with bearing wheels in front. A revolving steel disc on the side cuts the grass, and a small plowshare in the rear removes the cut sod.

The Philadelphia Grass-Edger has a set of revolving knives, put in motion by a bearing wheel to which is attached a handle. The operator pushes the wheel along the grass edge, the quick revolving knives cutting the projecting blades of grass, leaving the edges well shaved.

Richmond Sod Cutter.—This is an implement of recent introduction, and to landscape gardeners and others requiring sods in quantity, is of much value as a labor-saving appliance. Worked by one man and a horse, it is claimed that this machine will cut from thirty to forty thousand square feet of sod per day. In form it is a square box, supported by two small wheels, drawn by a horse, and guided by handles. A flat steel knife in front runs under the sod, cutting ribbons of uniform width and thickness.

Lawn Sprinklers.—The lawn sprinkler is a valuable invention for use on lawns and grass plots, in cities and villages where a supply of water under pressure can be had. The apparatus is made of a single gas pipe two and one-half or three feet long, standing upright, supported on cast-iron feet. Near the base of the pipe is a screw-opening for the attachment of a water hose. At the top arms are so fitted as to revolve by the force of water pressure; they are made hollow and perforated, and on the end generally have a perforated ball or bulb. As the arms revolve the water is thrown out centrifugally in a fine spray for a considerable distance. The number of arms vary; some machines have four, others six to eight. Several styles of small sprinklers adapted to more limited spaces are also made.

CHAPTER XXIV.

A Half-Acre Garden.

The quantity of seed required for a half acre, during the spring, and for a succession of those kinds requiring sowing at later periods, will not vary much from the following table:

> Beet in three varieties, eight ounces each.
> Beans, pole, two varieties, two quarts each.
> Beans, dwarf, three varieties, three quarts each.
> Corn, sugar, four varieties, one quart each.
> Cucumber, two varieties, eight ounces each.
> Carrots, two varieties, four ounces each.
> Celery, two varieties, four ounces each.
> Cabbage, three varieties, one ounce each.
> Lettuce, three varieties, four ounces each.
> Melon, Water, two varieties, two ounces each.
> Melon, Citron, two varieties, two ounces each.
> Parsnips, one variety, four ounces each.
> Radishes, three varieties, four ounces each.
> Squash, three varieties, four ounces each.
> Spinach, two varieties, eight ounces each.
> Tomatoes, three varieties, four ounces each.
> Herbs, four varieties, one ounce each.

In well managed gardens vegetable seeds are sown, or plants set out in rows, and to enable the amateur to make a close calculation of the quantity of various seeds required for any determined or measured area, the writer gives the following table, showing how much is needed for a row one hundred yards long. In these calculations, however, it is supposed that the seed are fresh, and that, at least, eighty per cent. will vegetate under favorable conditions.

A HALF-ACRE GARDEN.

To Sow One Hundred Yards.

Asparagus, eight ounces.
Beans, bush, three quarts.
Beans, lima, three pints.
Beans, pole, one pint.
Beet, five ounces.
Broccoli, one-half ounce.
Brussels sprouts, one-half ounce.
Cabbage, one ounce.
Carrot, three ounces.
Cauliflower, one-half ounce.
Celery, three ounces.
Collards, one-half ounce.
Corn, one pint.
Cress, four ounces.
Cucumber, four ounces.
Egg plant, one-half ounce.
Endive, two ounces.
Leek, two ounces.
Lettuce, two ounces.
Melon, Water, two ounces.
Melon, Citron, one ounce.
Mustard, four ounces.
Okra, twelve ounces.
Onion, two ounces for large bulbs.
Onion, eight ounces for sets.
Parsley, two ounces.
Parsnip, three ounces.
Peas, three quarts.
Pepper, one-half ounce.
Pumpkin, two ounces.
Radish, six ounces.
Rhubarb, four ounces.
Salsify, four ounces.
Spinach, six ounces.
Squash, three ounces.
Tomato, one ounce.
Turnips, three ounces.

The thoughtful cultivator will, as a necessary precaution, provide himself with a surplus quantity of the seeds he designs to plant, to hold as a reserve for replantings, as dry weather, beating rains and insect depredations often destroy the first sowings. The amateur gardener, and the expert, as well, should make out a list of the varieties of vegetables he desires to have, and then lay off on a paper a diagram of his garden, assigning certain rows to each sort. He can then readily calculate the amount of seed he will require.

Desirable Varieties.—Desirable varieties of the leading families of garden vegetables are named as follows, and in order of maturity for table:

BEANS.
Extra Early Red Valentine.
Pink Eye Wax.
Landreth's Scarlet.

CABBAGE.
Select Early Jersey Wakefield.
Reedland Early Drumhead.
Large Late Flat Dutch.

CARROT.
Blunt Horn.
Half Long Coreless.
Nantes Half Long.

LETTUCE.
Landreth's Forcing.
Reliable.
Largest of All.

WATERMELON.
Round Dark Icing.
Long Light Icing.
Boss.

CANTALOUPE.
Jenny Lind.
Extra Early Hackensack.
Acme.

PARSNIP.
Bloomsdale.

CAULIFLOWER.
Landreth's First.
Snowball.
Half Early Paris.

SUGAR CORN.
Early Minnesota.
Crosby.
Evergreen.

CELERY.
Dwarf White.
White Plume.
Paris Golden.

CELERIAC.
Apple shaped.

CUCUMBER.
Landreth First.
White Spine.
Long Green.

ONIONS.
Pearl.
Extra Early Red.
Silver Skin.

PEAS.
Landreth Extra Early.
Advancer.
Telephone.

RADISH.
Short Topped Earliest White.
Prussian Scarlet Globe.
Long Scarlet Strap Leaved.

SQUASH.
Extra Early Bush.
Yellow Summer Crook Neck.
Hubbard.

TOMATOES.
Extra Early Jersey.
Beauty.
Stone.

As it is always desirable, in a garden, to have a continuous and rapid succession of crops. A system of rotation must be studied out and followed, otherwise at certain seasons part of the garden will go uncropped, and a direct loss ensue, for it is only by attention to the details of a prompt succession of crops that any cash profit can be had out of a private garden.

CHAPTER XXV.

Calender Indicating Operations for the Northern and Southern States.

JANUARY.

NORTHERN.—January is unfavorable to out-door labor; in the garden, especially, but little can be done. In the orchard some work may be attempted. Rods for beans and peas may be made ready, manure collected, compost heaps formed,—and, by the way, compost is beyond all comparison the best shape in which to apply fertilizers to most vegetable crops. Fruit trees pruned, hedges clipped—those formed of evergreens not till frost has disappeared—shape them narrow at the top, wide at the base. Asparagus beds top-dressed with compost and salt preparatory to being dug when frost has ceased. Hot-beds for early forcing may be made ready.

SOUTHERN.—For the Southern States the writer simply aims to remind the reader of what may be done if the surroundings and climate be favorable. The enterprising man is not usually deterred by fears, and if his judgment leads him to take the risk, he may act upon some of the following suggestions, if he resides south of the latitude of Charleston. The market gardener in the lower part of the Florida Peninsula cultivates under conditions peculiar alone to his section.

Sow radishes sparsely from time to time. Dress asparagus beds with compost and salt. This latter, though an active agent, may be safely given in heavy dressings to asparagus, and has the further advantage of destroying weeds. Horseradish cuttings may be put out and peas sown at intervals; and if some are frosted, try again. For very early cabbage select Summer Flatbead and Early Jersey Wakefield,—these may be sown for Spring and early Summer use; the Reedland Early Drumhead may now be sown to come in still later; also the early Dwarf Flat Dutch, a variety which stands both heat and cold, and which can be highly commended—thus keeping up an uninterrupted succession. Cauliflower planted in the autumn will begin to head and may need slight protection at this season. Broccoli sown in September will begin to head, and it should be more widely cultivated. Sow turnips for early crop, also beets, carrots, spinach, parsley, all of which may be repeated next month. Hoe onions and other hardy crops planted in Autumn. Lettuce plants from fall sowings should be transplanted; celery earthed up as required; endive should now be in full growth, and tied up to blanch, in small quantities only as needed; garlic, shallots and onion sets may still be planted, and peas planted the last of the month.

FEBRUARY.

NORTHERN.—Next month will bring its work, and we can now only prepare for it. It is presumed that all persons residing in the country are provided with a cheap and simple hotbed, for forwarding tender vegetables. Towards the close of this month seeds of cabbage, cauliflower, tomato, egg plant and pepper may be planted in hotbed; watch them lest they suffer by frost, or, as is not infrequently the case, from want of sufficient air as the weather becomes milder, when they will need also increased watering.

If tools and implements are likely to be needed, the thoughtful man provides them in due season, overhauls his stock of seeds, and makes out a list of those which may be needed, to the end that they may be in hand before the time of sowing.

SOUTHERN.—The time for active labor in the Southern States is at hand. Plant peas, selecting the Extra Early, which is unquestionably the greatest bearer among the first early sorts, and is of fine flavor. Among the best peas following in succession are the American Wonder, Premium Gem and Advancer. Beans, cabbage and cauliflower seed and White Leaved collards may be sown. Remember, highly enriched and well-tilled soil will alone produce good crops of the cabbage tribe, which embraces the turnip and ruta baga. The cabbage plants from previous sowings should be transplanted, also lettuce plants. Sow spinach, radishes, carrots, parsnips, salsify and beets, and re-dress the asparagus beds. This delicious vegetable may be improved by the application of salt or refuse pickle, of which heavy dressings may be safely given. Plant squashes and melons. Do not be deterred from fear of loss by change of temperature; the gardener who counts every liability will be, in the main, behind his more enterprising neighbor. Plant Minnesota Sugar corn for the first crop, follow up with Crosby Sugar, Early Mammoth and Evergreen for succession. Plant early potatoes, Ohio or Rose.

MARCH.

NORTHERN.—Asparagus seed may be sown, or the roots set out. For early beets sow Eclipse, Philadelphia Turnip and Early Blood Turnip. Sow cabbage in a sheltered place, if not already in hotbed. Test Landreth's Earliest, Very Early Wakefield, Landreth's Early Summer Flathead, Early Market and Early Drumhead. Sow carrots, Extra Early Forcing cauliflower—attend to those under glass. Celery, cress, etc. Prepare compost and manure for late hotbeds. Set out horseradish plants, make hotbeds, sow and transplant lettuce. Attend to mushroom beds and sow mustard. For onions put out as sets, those known as "Philadelphia Buttons" keep the best. Of parsnips, Bloomsdale is the best. Peas, Extra Early, Advancer, Premium Gem. Plant early potatoes; the Early Ohio is a prolific early. Sow Market Gardeners' and Summer White radish; the Strap-leaved Long Scarlet is an improvement on the old Long Scarlet, and is recommended. Sow rhubarb or plant roots. Sow seed of garden sage and tomatoes in hot-bed; Early Jersey ripens first. Sow turnips, but generally so far north as Philadelphia these directions will apply better to April than to March.

SOUTHERN.—Southward of Washington. Continue to plant peas and beans; Landreth's Scarlet is a fine golden wax. Transplant cabbage plants from winter beds, especially Landreth's Earliest, also Jersey Wakefield. Remember to have fine head cabbage and lettuce; deep culture and highly manured soil is required. Sow Extra Early Red onion and Extra Early Yellow. Leeks may be sown and a few turnips. Plant potatoes. Sow carrots and parsnips, if enough were not sown last month. Mustard and Cutting lettuce, for small salad, should be sown at least once a fortnight. Sow parsley and tomatoes in warm situation; those from the hotbed may be set out. Sow peppers at the close of this month. Watermelons—Boss and Long Light Icing—may be planted, also Extra Early and Acme cantaloupe, and Reedland Giant muskmelon. Cucumbers, First and Choice; Okra, Landreth's Long Green Pod; also squash and pumpkins. Beets and other root crops sown last month will be advancing; they should be thinned and cultivated. Sow celery—Paris Golden, and Spinach. Dress asparagus beds if not already done, and set out strawberry beds. French artichokes, if slipped and dressed last month, should have attention.

APRIL.

NORTHERN.—The exact time at which certain seeds should be sown must depend not only on location in respect to latitude, but also on the nature of the soil; if it be heavy, a little delay will rather promote than retard our object; the common sense of each one must be used.

Sow asparagus seed or plant roots, if not attended to last month. Wherever practicable, a bed of sufficient size should be made to permit an ample supply without cutting every feeble shoot which peeps above the surface; indeed where space and means admit, two beds should be maintained, and cut alternate seasons. Plant Landreth's Scarlet and Pink Eye Wax beans. Beets, Early and Long. Cabbage, Reedland, Early Drumhead and Late Flat Dutch; sow freely that there be enough for the fly and to plant out. Carrots, Extra Early Forcing, and Danvers. Celery, if not sown last month; aim for large plants. Cress and cucumbers, sow in warm spot. Plant horseradish, if not done. Sow leeks and lettuce in drills, also plant from beds of last autumn's sowing. Sow sweet marjoram and mustard for salad. Sow nasturtiums and onions, and plant buttons for table use and for sets; sow white, red and yellow thickly. Sow parsley; parsnips, Bloomsdale Sugar; peas, early and late, for a succession. Plant potatoes; Green Mountain is a variety of very superior quality. Sow radish, Earliest White, Prussian Golden Globe, White Summer and Lady-finger, for succession. Sow salsify, sage and spinach, at short intervals; also thyme and tomatoes on borders, to succeed those sown in hotbeds. Sow turnips, if not sown last month; they may succeed.

SOUTHERN.—Spring sown cabbage will now be fit to transplant; manure well, if you expect fine heads. The plants set out in February and March will require culture, and deep tillage is demanded by the cabbage tribe.

About the middle or latter end of this month, sow Reedland Early, Late Mountain, Late Flat Dutch, Late Drumhead, Flat Dutch and Drumhead Savoy cabbage seed, for plants to be set out in June. Cauliflower and broccoli may be sown. Carrots, parsnips and beets previously sown are now advancing in growth, and should receive necessary care; additional sowings of each may now be made. Pearl onions, set out in autumn, should be fit for use. Sow leeks for winter use. Turnips sown last month should be hoed and thinned. Draw up the earth to the potato vines. Sow radishes; the White Summer and Golden Globe are the best for the season. Lettuce may be drilled where intended to head. Sow celery; plant more cucumbers, melons and squashes. Study varieties. The fertilizer best adapted to these vines is compost prepared the past season, formed of decomposed manure, well rotted sod, wood earth, etc. It is sufficiently stimulating, and will not be likely to burn the plants during dry weather, and the vines will bear better than when of more rampant growth. Sow okra, Long Green Pod, if not already in. The vigilant gardener will keep his eye upon the weeds.

MAY.

NORTHERN.— During the past month the hardier vegetables have been sown, and by the middle of the present month all will have been put in.

Plant bush beans for succession; Lima, Carolina, and other pole beans may now be planted. Sow Long beets. Plant cabbage, and sow seed if not done last month. Plant peppers. Sow Nantes carrot. Remove glass in cauliflower frames. Weed celery. Repeat sowings for crops which have failed when first sown. Plant Jersey Pickle cucumbers. Sow Reliable lettuce, Largest of All, and Dutch Butter, in drills to stand; thin out to four inches. Plant melons; the best are the Boss and

Long Light Icing. Among musk melons the Extra Early is the first to ripen, but is not as good as many others; Acme is a good variety. Thin out parsnips, if ready.

SOUTHERN.—Plant pole beans, Lima, Carolina and Creaseback; also Dwarf Pink Eye Wax. The Saddleback is good. Sow cabbage for winter; sow lettuce, Landreth's Cutting and Golden Curled. Sow radishes, the Golden Globe and White Summer. Melons, cucumbers and squashes may be put in. Plant Landreth's Sugar and Evergreen corn, for succession. Sow peppers and tomatoes for plants for later crops. Set out sweet potatoes in suitable weather. Where water is of easy application it may answer to supply it, otherwise it hardly pays the cost of the labor. Under a burning sun, water should not be given directly; it is better to apply it between rows of plants, they will thus supply themselves without the liability to scald.

JUNE.

NORTHERN.—The labors of the gardener will mainly consist in the tillage of the growing crop. The rapid growth of weeds at this season will admonish him of the necessity of timely exertion.

The aid of appropriate tools in the culture of crops and the extermination of weeds need not be commended. Good implements are indispensable to success, and he who has provided them will not only have greater pleasure in his labors, but the profit which attends the judicious application of both time and labor.

Keep asparagus beds clean. Plant Bush or Bunch beans for succession, and cultivate those in growth. Thin beets to four inches. Plant out broccoli, those sown in April; also cabbages, especially the sorts which it is desired shall come into use in September and October, in advance of the winter varieties. Plant out celery, a portion for early use. Sow successive crops of cucumbers, of choice varieties. Plant Early Mammoth Sugar corn for a succession. Sow endive. Thin or transplant leeks. A few peas may be planted as a succession.

SOUTHERN.—Plant beans; transplant cabbage and cauliflower, and Spring-heading broccoli seed may be sown. Cucumbers, melons and squashes may be planted. Sow tomatoes for a succession, beginning with the Early Jersey, Acme and Perfection. The chief labor in the garden had better be directed to what is already in growth; but few seeds sown in hot weather, in a Southern climate, repay the trouble.

JULY.

NORTHERN.—This, like June, is the month of labor in the garden. Weeds are in rapid growth, plants are to be set out, and various matters require attention.

Plant Landreth's Scarlet beans for succession; beets, the stock-feeding varieties, Long Blood Sugar; mangold wurtzel may be planted for stock as late as the first of July. June is, however, much better. Beets, Early Blood Red Turnip, and half Long for late winter and spring use, may be sown. The winter sorts of cabbage should now be planted out; where many are to be transplanted it is best to wait for a suitable time, a heavy rain or showery weather; but in a small garden cabbages may be transplanted at almost any season by careful watering, and, if need be, shading. Plant celery. Sow endive. A few peas may be sown, but they seldom do well at this season. Turnips of all kinds may be sown.

SOUTHERN.—Under favorable conditions, plant beans. Transplant cabbage, cauliflower, and broccoli. Transplant leeks. Sow Nantes carrots and parsnips. Sow endive for early crop. A few turnips may be sown. Transplant celery for early supply, and prepare trenches for the main crop. Spinach may be sown toward the close of the month. The seed will not vegetate if the ground be dry; watering is practiced by some, but the results scarcely repay the labor. Plant white potatoes. Short Prolific and Jersey Pickle cucumbers may be planted for pickles. Our remarks on ruta bagas apply with increased force, for in the South pasturage is less abundant than in the North; besides, it is a most wholesome food for man as well as beast.

Usually at this season the extreme heat and prevailing drouth render it difficult to get seed to vegetate. If failures occur, the only remedy is to try again under more favorable circumstances. Much depends on the quality of the seed sown. The stale stuff not unfrequently sold, only disappoints and annoys. Therefore, purchase American grown, and that only the product of reliable persons, obtained direct or through merchants who get their supplies from the best sources and irrespective of price. That offered "remarkably cheap" is usually dear in the end.

AUGUST.

NORTHERN.—The work of this month does not vary materially from the month just closed. Cabbage, for winter use, may head if planted at once. Earth up celery, and plant for future use. Plant endive. Bush or Snap beans gathered late in autumn, may be preserved in brine (salt and water) for winter use, and vary but little from those freshly gathered. Sow Forcing and Reliable lettuce, in drills to head. Sow peas, for this vegetable is a delicacy in autumn, and should more frequently appear at table. Extra Early, sown later or at end of this month and beginning of next, will perfect before frost. Sow Bloomsdale spinach for autumn use; for winter use, sow next month. Sow the Spanish and China radishes for winter, and the Golden Globe and

Red Turnip rooted for autumn use. Sow ruta bagas without delay, if not already done. Should the ground be dry, work thoroughly and sow in the dust: the seed may vegetate with the first shower. A roller to compress the soil sometimes promotes vegetation; but there is this disadvantage, if heavy, dashing rain immediately ensues, the ground packs, and the seed is lost. Yellow Aberdeen, Pomeranean Globe and Amber Globe turnips should be sown early in the month; also the Sweet German turnip. Early Dutch and Red-topped may be sown until first of September, though it will do well to sow at least a portion earlier, as at a late day it is difficult to remedy a failure.

SOUTHERN.—Sow Reedland Early Drumhead cabbage seed, to head in November; also Landreth's Earliest, Early Jersey Wakefield, Bloomsdale Early Market and Early Dwarf Flat Dutch for family use. Sow broccoli and cauliflower, and transplant from an earlier sowing. Sow White Leaved collards. Plant onion sets for autumn. Sow carrots, squashes and ruta bagas to make up deficiencies in July sowing. Sow turnips for table use at short intervals. Plant potatoes for winter use. Drill lettuce. Sow radishes from time to time. Beets may be sown for the winter supply. Seeds directed to be sown this month, it may, perhaps be necessary to defer until the next, by reason of heat and drouth. Let the young gardener be not disheartened; ultimately success will attend persevering efforts.

SEPTEMBER.

NORTHERN.—Many and varied are the duties which devolve upon the gardener at this season. Not only do the growing crops demand attention, but seeds are to be sown to provide the necessary plants for the ensuing Spring. Roots are to be divided and reset; strawberries planted. Sow Landreth's Earliest, Select Jersey Wakefield, and Reedland Early Drumhead cabbage, to plant out in autumn, where the locality admits, or box up in cold frame to keep until planting time in spring; the latter end of the month will be time enough to sow in the latitude of Philadelphia; especially sow the Early Market, also the Bloomsdale, as a succession. The Early Dutch and Red Topped turnips may be sown the first week in this month, if failure has attended earlier efforts. In some sections the fly devours the early sowing; they are less voracious after the nights become cool and dews heavy. Earth up celery. Sow corn salad, scurvy grass and chervil for winter salad. Sow Speckled Dutch lettuce for Spring planting, the plants to be kept during the Winter in cold frames. Other good sorts for autumn sowing are the Forcing, Reliable, and. Early Summer. Sow spinach early in the month for autumn use; later for winter and spring. The Bloomsdale is unquestionably the hardiest for winter, and withal the best in leaf.

SOUTHERN.—The work in the garden has commenced in earnest. It is not too late to plant beans. Transplant cabbage sown last month; Early Market, Early Dwarf Flat Dutch, Reedland Early Drumhead, also the Early Jersey Wakefield, may still be sown.

Towards the close of this and the fore part of next month, sow Flat Dutch, Lake Mountain, and Drumhead Savoy cabbage, for use early in the Spring, and to secure a good supply, sow liberally—the flies will have their share. Transplant cauliflower and broccoli, and sow turnips. Potatoes planted last month will require culture. Bloomsdale onion seed may be sown for a general crop, if Buttons or sets to plant are not at hand. Get sets of Pearl, Autumn, White Wax and Bermuda onions, Carrots sown now will be fit for use in December. Spinach may be sown from time to time; also endive. Celery plants need tillage. Lettuce may be sown, and Landreth's Forcing is a rare sort. Sow radishes frequently; especially winter radishes.

OCTOBER.

NORTHERN.—The labors of the gardener are varied, and he who neglects duties necessary to be done loses time not to be regained; the autumn is upon him. The principal labors are, the protection of crops already grown, and transplanting others. Top-dress asparagus beds. Set out cabbage plants in a sheltered location and on light land for next season's use. Store beets and carrots now or early next month. Plant out lettuce for next spring, and dig potatoes. Sow spinach at once, if not sown last month. Plant the Bloomsdale variety, as it is hardiest.

SOUTHERN.—Beans, planted last month, should be cultivated. Transplant cabbage, also cauliflower and broccoli. Set out Bloomsdale Pearl onion sets and Autumn White Wax; these varieties are, indeed, wonderful for early maturity, size and appearance. Plant garlic and eschalots. Sow spinach for winter use. Earth up celery in dry weather, and transplant from seed bed for further supplies; also lettuce for spring use. Sow radishes as required. Dress artichokes preparatory for winter. Dress asparagus beds. Transplant strawberries.

NOVEMBER.

NORTHERN.—The season for gardening is drawing to a close; indeed, it is limited to the preservation of roots and the hardier vegetables for winter use, and such operations as may be preparatory to another season. Now is a good time to transplant fruit and ornamental trees, shrubbery, etc. On loamy and light land, we prefer, decidedly, fall planting, but on heavy soil, or where the subsoil is clay, thus retaining the moisture near the surface, spring may be a more favorable season; and it is generally esteemed the best for evergreens. Dress asparagus beds. Dig beets and store. Place cabbages in safe quarters. Dig carrots and store. Earth up celery finally. Drain vacant ground if needful. Dig horseradish and store for convenience. Examine onions in store. Dig and pit parsnips and salsify for convenient access. From first to twentieth of this month, according to locality, the winter supply of turnips should be pulled and pitted.

SOUTHERN.—The garden work is ample enough to occupy attention. Sow peas; if they escape the frost they will be ready for use in April. For sowing at this season, we recommend Tom Thumb and American Wonder; they seldom rise over twelve inches, are abundant bearers, and are, withal, quite early; also Little Gem, the three seeming to be admirably adapted to autumn sowing in the South, where, on apprehended frost, protection may be given; they are also equally well suited to early spring planting for the same reason, and if planted on ground manured excessively high, will yield as much to a given quantity of land as any pea known to us. Set out cabbage, if plants remain. Plant Pearl, Autumn White Wax and Bermuda onion sets. Blanch celery. Sow salad on sheltered spots. Sow radishes; if frost kills them, it is only a little labor lost.

DECEMBER.

NORTHERN.—Prepare compost. Prepare dung for hotbeds. Attend to hotbeds. Sow radish and cauliflower salad in frames. Trench and drain vacant ground. Transplanting trees may still be done.

SOUTHERN.—In the far South, peas may be sown to succeed those of November. See remarks under that head. Cabbage plants, sown in October, will be fit to put out. Sow Landreth's Earliest, Select Jersey Wakefield, and Reedland Early Drumhead, to head in January and February. Sow radishes and lettuce. Look over the spinach, thin it as you collect for daily use. Onion sets of all kinds may now be planted. Prepare ground for carrots. Earth up celery in dry weather. Tie up endive. Prune fruit trees, vines, etc. Transplant all hardy trees.

CHAPTER XXVI.

The Grass Question.

A multitude of farmers in the corn-growing States, and a still greater number in the cotton States of this country, are in quest of profitable and reliable tame grasses. In an agricultural sense, under the designation "grass" is included the true grasses and those other forage and hay-making plants sown in connection with grass, and termed artificial grasses, as Red Clover, Alfalfa, Sainfoin, Trefoil, and others.

It may be stated, in a general way, that the capacity of land to grow desirable grasses is the measure of its agricultural value, and the extent and success in the practice of growing grass indicates the degree of advancement of a farmer in the scale of merit. Without grass, although he may produce some poor stringy beef, he cannot grow good mutton nor wool, nor will he have plenty of hay. In the South, particularly, as an outgrowth of plenty of good hay and liberal feeding, that important farm manufactory known as the barnyard would be seen on a half million farms, which never knew a barnyard in its practical sense, as a manufactory for manure. The farm, county or State which cannot produce its own pasturage for spring, summer and autumn, and its own hay for winter, is only half way up in the agricultural scale, be its other crops ever so profitable, for it is dependent on other sections for an agricultural staple which it should itself produce.

In locations where such protracted drouth prevails as to burn up the present standard perennial grass, there are badly needed other varieties of grasses which will resist drouth, and, remaining green under hot sun, continue to furnish a nutritious bite when others have succumbed. Bermuda grass, a perennial from the West Indies, to some extent fills the requirements, but it has the objectionable characteristic of sometimes making itself a nuisance by its persistence.

While the test of years and the experience of nations point to certain perennial varieties of grass as standards on ordinary farming soils, it sometimes occurs that wild or native sorts have high merit in their respective locality. For instance, many of the so-called wild annual grasses of the Southern States, so frequently looked upon by the planter as nuisances, especially those that strive to take possession of cultivated fields during conditions of summer heat, almost deadly to standard varieties of grass and other farm crops, are, many of them, even though some be annual sorts, just the types to carry coarse-wooled sheep through such trying seasons, conditions more serious to contemplate than the finding of winter subsistence. For, in respect to winter feeding of sheep or other cattle, the South has a great advantage over the North in possessing a climate encouraging grass to grow almost continuously, an elimination, to a large extent, from the costs of sheep husbandry of the Northern expenses of housing the animals, and the storage and cost of prolonged winter feeding.

The physical characteristics of grasses must be studied by the thoughtful farmer as respects their adaptability to his special soils, climate and purpose; for instance, varieties doing well on dry land should not be sown on heavy, low, damp situations, nor others affording a luxuriant and nutritious feed for pastured cattle, but of a habit of forming high tussocks, should not be sown with the expectation of machine mowing; nor, again, should other sorts specially adapted to cutting green and feeding in the pen or stable, but which, like Alfalfa, have their crowns so elevated above the earth level as to be nibbled off by sheep, be sown for sheep grazing.

Profitable farming in the Southern States can best be developed and diversified by diverting from the ordinary system of cultivation, or worse neglect, large areas to pasturage, and hay fields of Blue grass, Clover, Alfalfa, Alsike and Incarnatum, or, better, in some locations wild grasses, thus enabling planters to feed some millions of sheep and clip six times as many millions of pounds of unwashed wool, supplemental to which would follow an extended culture in corn and oats.

It is self-evident that, to realize the wealth which millions of sheep, with their mutton and wool, would add to the South, there must be less acreage in cotton and a greater acreage in grass, for, while Mexican sheep, having some of the qualities of the goat, may live on such stuff as thistles and cactus, the finer-bred sheep must have an ample supply of succulent grass, with hay, corn and oats. There is an old proverb which is very true, "No grass, no cattle; no cattle, no manure; no manure, no crops;" or, to illustrate the idea in other language, there is a French proverb, that grass is a synonym for bread, beef, mutton and clothing.

Sheep farming naturally follows an advance in grass farming, but the grass must be provided before the sheep. When obtained, the two preserve the fertility of good lands, and, under good management, restore those classed as unfertile, and enrich the State. Nearly every farm of two hundred acres of arable land can support a flock of thirty to forty sheep, and, if it is not in condition to do so, its owner should not rest till, with clover, corn, rye and other green manures, he has brought up his farm to that desirable condition.

The American farmer need have little fear of overproduction of wool, as the annual consumption in the United States amounts to 600,000,000 pounds of unwashed wool, which may be estimated as the clip from 100,000,000 sheep. The Census Bureau of 1890 gives the total number of sheep in the United States as 43,000,000, of a value of $116,000,000, and cutting 290,000,000 pounds of unwashed wool.

In connection with the extension of grass culture on poor lands, much may be said in favor of green manuring as a preparation of lands, to sustain a crop of grass. For example, it often occurs that thin soils, which, without the expensive stimulus of commercial fertilizers, will not develop a fair sod of the standard perennial grasses, will yet grow a passable spring crop of broadcasted corn to a height of two or three feet. This plowed down before midsummer, and the field again immediately broadcasted with a second sowing of corn, to be plowed down in autumn, and followed by a broadcasted crop of rye, to be plowed down in February or March, will be found to have a marvellous fertilizing effect in sustaining grass, or any other crop. The man who pursues such a course of rejuvenation of his land should have his taxes remitted, for he is a good example in any locality, and should be encouraged. The corn and rye system of green manuring supersedes the slow process of clover renovation. Cultivated grasses of biennial habit are, few of them, after being down for several years, entirely able to take care of themselves, but must be assisted by harrowing and seeding on bare spots, top dressing with fertilizer, and rolling. Worn-out pastures can be renovated, to a marked degree, by the application of bone phosphates, dried fish, meat and blood, and the nitrate salts. Of late, in Europe, much attention has been directed to the use of a new fertilizer known as slag phosphate, a by-product of the Basic process of making Bessemer steel. This slag phosphate seems especially adapted for grass, and its trial is recommended.

In many localities the profits of grass land can be increased over fourfold by means of irrigation, and its practice should unquestionably be pursued when the conditions are favorable; that is, when water in large volume may be cheaply obtained, which, flowing by gravity from more elevated sources, can be distributed beneath the surface by underground conductors, in open ditches, or upon the surface. The writer once visited the irrigated farms outside of Bedford, England, and was amazed at the grass development. Subsequently, visiting Barking, below London, he saw crops of rye grown which produced a fresh cutting every three weeks of ten tons to the acre. He was informed that one hundred tons of green rye grass had been cut to the acre, in a single summer.

While irrigation, in parts of the West, and on the Pacific slope, is a thing of everyday agricultural practice, enforced by reason of climatic conditions, and cheaply practiced by reason of elevated water supplies, the system is almost unknown in the rainfall States. Few localities can draw cheap and plentiful supplies of water from mountain sides, but even under the expense of pumping from rivers, it will pay to do it on tracts sufficiently large and level for the advantageous distribution of water.

Over three thousand varieties of plants of the grass family are known and described by botanists, and while by far the greater part are of such character as at once to remove them from the list of farm forage plants, there remains a vast number not cultivated, scarcely tested, but worthy of experiment. The list of seeds of forage grasses offered by European seed merchants at the present day numbers over two hundred annual, biennial and perennial varieties; but, without doubt, the number will, ere long, be considerably extended, for there are many wild forms of grasses all over the world well worthy of propagation; for example, some of the wild grasses of Texas, Arizona and the Southwestern plains, rich when green, and very nutritious in the form of self-dried hay. Many of these may be much improved by critical selection, hybridization and rich feeding, and be fitted for cultivation in all high dry altitudes of the cotton belt. Among these wild grasses of the plains the most common is the Grama grass, a perennial on the heavier soils, and known botanically as *Bouteloua oligostachya*. It is found on all the great plains of the Southwest, growing in low, cushion-like masses, forming a succession of tussocks—a habit rendering it unsuitable for mowing, even if it grew tall enough for hay, which it does not. As a pasturage grass it is highly nutritious, and cures good hay on its own root.

The next widely distributed variety on the prairie is the Buffalo grass, known as *Buchloë dactyloides*, a native of the plains from Texas up to Missouri. It is a perennial, affording a reliable supply of forage. In dry locations it is desirable as a lawn grass. It is of low habit, seldom rising over four inches, and is inclined to grow in tufts, or patches. It is found in greatest breadths on the Texas prairies in the vicinity of Mesquit trees, hence it is often called Mesquit grass. It possesses a runner of long creeping habit, and, once established on congenial soil, soon spreads over the adjacent land. Bearing few seeds, it is, consequently, best propagated by cuttings. When green, it is sweet and nutritious, and, dried as hay on the root, is very palatable to cattle. During drouths, when appearing to be about dead, it springs into life upon a rain, becoming green in a few hours, and developing with phenomenal rapidity.

Either of these grasses, no doubt, can, by selection, be improved as respects productiveness and durability—they are not referred to as the only ones, or the best ones, but as examples of sorts already pastured upon by millions of horses, cattle and sheep. Why should not these and others be brought to the Southeastern States, as most efficient aids in the diversification of agricultural practice?

Another American perennial grass not generally known, but of admirable character for Southern sections, is the Texas Blue grass (*Poa arachnifera*) discovered on the prairies of that State in 1853. It blossoms there about the last of March, and ripens its seed about the middle of April. Its habit, in Southern States, is much stronger than Kentucky Blue grass. In Texas, under the severest drouths, it sometimes lags a little, but, after autumn rains, quickly springs into most vigorous growth, and continues to grow all winter. It makes a strong top growth for hay, and a matted sod standing continued pasturing. It roots deeply and spreads rapidly by buds from long, strong, underground stems, which, by their vigor, resist the encroachment of Bermuda grass. Once established, it will continue to stand for a lifetime. It is best propagated by cuttings of the roots, 20,000 set to the acre, or, say, one to each two square feet. Six pounds of seed are sown to the acre.

These, and other grasses, will, before long, be brought into general cultivation, indeed, all of our cultivated grasses are selections from wild forms; no doubt very inferior, originally; for instance, Timothy, now the leading hay grass north of the cotton belt, was found growing wild in the hilly or mountainous districts, by the early American colonists, and sent to England in 1763, where it at once assumed the highest rank over the four or five kinds of grasses then cultivated. Indeed, up to 1815, only four or five kinds were cultivated, and it was not until the list of grasses was largely increased and root culture extended, that British agriculture began to develop, for not till then were there increased opportunities for the extension of grazing and the winter subsistence of cattle. Red Top is another American grass, first cultivated about 1760, by the colonists. It was soon followed by the introduction to cultivation of Kentucky Blue grass, and, subsequently, Orchard grass.

It will be noticed that the United States furnished four out of the five principal hay and pasturage producers used in agricultural practice; the fourth, Red Clover, being a native of Asia. It cannot be doubted that there yet remain others to be brought into cultivation.

An observation of the varieties of grasses blooming in a pasture will not serve to determine the quality of the sward, for cattle, eating off the most palatable sorts, prevent them from reaching a condition of inflorescence. Thus, those valuable varieties which perpetuate themselves by seed, sometimes tend to run out, leaving the field to the more unpalatable sorts, but not always, for nature provides, in the cases of some grasses, that varieties not reaching a condition of seed-bearing, shall perpetuate themselves by abnormal root budding.

Much can be determined of the components of a pasturage sward by a study of the structural character of the plants, even when grazed down to one inch. In Germany so much attention has been paid to the analysis of pasturage grasses and the description of varieties, that the subject is no longer a novel one. By such analyses, perennial grasses are distinguished from annual by the crowns and roots; crowns of perennial varieties bearing relics of the preceding year's growth, while to the roots are attached creeping underground bud stems. A third test can be made by dissection of the stalks, for in perennials only a few embryo flowers will be found, while among annual varieties every shoot will contain an embryo flower.

It is equally easy to recognize the leading varieties, even if closely eaten down, by examination of their base sheaths and general lower developments. For example: Perennial Rye grass possesses a flat sheath, very red, and leaves strongly ribbed, with ears at the base; veins just discernible, even when held up between the eye and the light. Meadowy Fescue has a round sheath, decidedly red, leaves strongly ribbed, veins on leaves clearly marked as white lines, upon examination by transmitted light. Crested Dogtail possesses a half flat sheath, quite yellow, leaves never eared. At base of leaves a collar-like growth, peaked into two ear-like terminals. Foxtail, a flat sheath of deep violet color, almost black, leaf ribs flat.

Timothy has the base enlarged to a green, bulb-like growth, similar to a small, very hard onion. At the junction of the sheath and blade there is found a thin white membrane, with sharp white teeth on the top. Blue grass has a flat, elliptical sheath, light colored leaves, with round ends, parallel sides and rounded base, fleshy, hard and ribless, of a dark color under transmitted light. Orchard grass has the sheath broad and flat, leaves ribbed, with prominent keel on the under surface; conspicuous thin white membrane at top of sheath. Red Top is more variable than any of the preceding. The sheath is without color, leaves rolled thin and dry, rough on both sides, ribs prominent, margin of leaves converged at base, never eared.

Regarding compounded mixtures of grass seeds, it has been frequently stated that seedsmen advocate mixed grasses for lawn and pasturage, that they may have an opportunity to run up the price. This is a mistake, for no pasture grass mixture is so costly as the same measure of pure Blue grass, the basis of all good grazing mixtures. Let it be understood, the object of mixing varieties of grass seeds is manifold; for instance, to insure a more numerous stand of plants, for some varieties may germinate better than others; then, again, that some varieties be succulent and bright, when others are dingy, and for pasturage this is a very important consideration. Another good reason is, that soils vary so much and seasons vary so much, that it is best, in seeding down a pasturage, to diversify the risks.

The deliberate mixing of distinct varieties of vegetable or flower seeds is looked upon, by all men, as a fraud of the worst kind, but the intelligent mixing of distinct varieties of grass seeds is an art which should be encouraged, for, properly done, it is in the interest of agriculture's most important crop—green pasturage and hay. Upon the length of time which it is contemplated to allow the pasturage to stand, depends, to a large extent, the varieties of grass seeds to mix, as, for example, Timothy, Italian Rye grass, Cocksfoot, White and Alsike clover are all very quick to develop, and suitable for a two or three years' shift, while, for a longer term, should be added Blue grass, Red Top, Foxtail, Tall Fescue, Perennial Rye, Lucerne and Red clover.

While the limestone soils of Kentucky and Tennessee will sustain, in full vigor, a pure Blue grass pasturage for a lifetime, few soils in other localities will be found equal to the task. On soils not suited to Blue grass alone, good temporary pasturage of two to five years' duration can be obtained, with a careful selection of varieties and satisfactory results, realized under a well-considered system of rotation. When one departs from the usual course of sowing Timothy with winter grain, to be followed with Clover in the spring, it is not a cheap matter to lay down a perfect pasture, hay field or lawn, for the preparation of the land is expensive, and a combination of varieties generally more costly than the simple varieties of Timothy and Clover.

In laying down a pasture field, it is best to do it in the autumn, if conditions of moisture will permit, for the reason that time is then less precious; but spring seeding, when the land is thoroughly prepared, is quite as effective. All prescriptions for grass seed mixtures, however, are little more than generalities, for no one can compile a table or series of tables, showing the varieties positively adapted to different localities, for soils, even on adjoining fields, frequently vary so much as to require an entire change in the varieties and proportions. How much more difficult to prescribe for unknown soils, some, perhaps, a thousand miles away.

The geological constitution, rainfall, drainage, altitude and objects sought, whether for hay or grazing, all need to be studied. The best guide is the experience of others in one's location, but even that is often misleading, for we have grown grand crops of Timothy and Clover in a section of a Southern State, where the farmers seldom saved any hay, trusting almost entirely to corn fodder—of course, there were no barnyards worthy of the name, in that locality. As an example, for ordinary soils a pasturage mixture might consist of forty pounds to the acre of Timothy, Orchard, Blue grass, Red Top, Perennial Rye grass and Red clover. Such a combination would be pretty certain to effect a stand, and, when once established, would comprehend some one variety in luxuriant growth throughout the extent of the growing season.

Of course, in special locations, as on lowlands or mountain sides, or on special soils, as sands, gravels, clays, loams, some of the named sorts might, with advantage, be omitted, and others added. Timothy, for example, a short-lived hay grass, does best on well-drained land, and in northern latitudes. Red Top, a longer-lived sort, does better on moist land, even sustaining long-continued overflow. Orchard grass, on the other hand, a good, all-around sort, will grow on dry, sandy loam; fairly well on poor clay, and better on rich bottoms, so it be not overflowed, and it even endures the shade of trees. Blue grass, doing best on limestone soils, is not a good hay producer, as it is a light cropper, difficult to cut, and harder to cure, but it is eminently a pasturage and lawn grass. It is an easy grower, flourishing for a limited time on gravels, bottoms and clays, while on limestone soils, grazing fields have been known to remain in perfection for sixty years. It will not stand severe drouth, but resists any amount of frost, while continued pasturage only makes it better.

Thin seeding of grass is a most serious mistake, as a poor stand of grass only leaves room for weeds to occupy the space. Consequently, we advise a very liberal application of seed, for, under the best conditions, as respects preparation of land, distribution of seed and covering, a large portion of the seed will get too deeply covered over to vegetate. Not more than one farmer in a hundred, by his field practice, shows any indication that he realizes the necessity of shallow covering of grass seeds, for they generally put on a harrow and cover, to a depth of one to two and one-half inches, delicate seeds not one-thirtieth of an inch in diameter. Certainly the greater part never shows a green blade, for farmers seldom stop to consider the delicate nature of the seeds they commit to rough, cloddy earth. One who sets himself to estimate the number of seeds in a pound, will soon come to a realization of the necessity for a perfect seed bed, for he will find the seeds to number, in a pound of Tall Fescue, 250,000, Red clover 280,000, Orchard grass 600,000, Timothy 1,250,000, Blue grass 2,375,000, Rough Meadow 3,000,000, and Red Top 8,000,000. Can it be expected that over ten per cent. of the seeds ever make a plant, considering the rough tillage and careless sowing of the ordinary farmer?

If one of an inquiring mind takes up a sod from a perfect grass pasturage and dissects it, he will find about six or seven distinct plants to every square inch, or eight hundred plants to the square foot, being about thirty-five millions to the acre. To obtain such a thick stand sufficient seed must be applied, or there will exist vacancies for the establishment of weeds. It may be interesting to enter into a calculation of how many seeds will be applied to an acre in thirty pounds of a mixture consisting of:

Number of Pounds.	No. Seeds to Pound.	Total Seeds.
Timothy, Five............	1,250,000	6,250,000
Orchard, Five............	600,000	3,000,000
Red Top, Five............	8,000,000	40,000,000
Blue grass, Ten...........	5,500,000	25,000,000
Red Clover, Five..........	280,000	1,400,000
A grand total of.....		75,650,000

Not less than an application of this number, of over seventy-five millions of seeds, can be relied upon to properly clothe an acre, an enormous number of seeds failing to make plants by reason of want of vitality, or on account of inefficient tillage or sowing. While the preceding table, drawn for purposes of calculation, might serve as a fair prescription, the writer would suggest the following as covering a wide variety of seasons of growth, and better as respects reproduction and duration: Blue grass, ten pounds; Orchard, ten pounds; Perennial Rye grass, four pounds; Meadow Fox Tail, four pounds; Red Top, three pounds; Timothy, three pounds; White clover, three pounds; Red clover, three pounds, or forty pounds in all.

For lawns, either for surface effect, or designed to resist tramping, or on athletic grounds, a mixture is required, differing in each case, and both quite distinct from that applied to pasturage or hay. A word upon lawn-making may not be out of place, for the seedsman is often blamed for bad seed, when the failure is the result of a neglect of proper precautions to insure success; as much of the success of lawn-making depends upon the preparation of the ground. The land must be well plowed, or dug and harrowed, or raked, to secure thorough pulverization, and after being reduced to a perfectly even surface, should be cleared of stumps, stones, roots and other impediments. The soil, if not wet, should then be made firm with a heavy roller, and top-dressed with a good fertilizer, unless the land had received an application of seven to eight tons of very short, well-rotted stable manure before plowing. We will here remark that stable manure is the best of all fertilizers, but there being some difficulty in obtaining it, and objections to its use, on account of its offensive appearance and smell, we recommend a good grade of concentrated commercial fertilizer. Six to seven hundred pounds to the acre of such mixture should be applied. The fertilizer should be lightly harrowed in upon the seedbed, as it will be lost to the young plants if buried much beneath the surface. After the harrowing, the ground should be severely rolled, that the earth and seed may be brought into close contact. The lawn grass mixture should be sown at the rate of forty pounds to the acre, and rolled down. Sowing in September and October will be found most advantageous in latitudes south of Philadelphia; in more northerly locations spring sowing is most successfully practiced, the work being done in April and May.

Annual seeds, natural to the soil, are certain to spring up before the young grass becomes established, and an inexperienced person is likely to conclude that the weeds spring from weed seed in the grass seed, but all soils contain weed seeds, and, upon tillage, they are certain to vegetate. The weeds, as they become large enough, may be cut down or pulled up; after the first year their growth will cease. Frequent rolling is advantageous in producing a good lawn, by solidifying the soil, harassing insects and other vermin, and improving the level of the surface. On all lawns will regularly appear, in greater or less numbers, certain interlopers, such as Buttercups, Plantains, Dandelions, all from seeds natural to the soil. These uninvited guests should always be dug out, otherwise subsequent labor will be increased one hundred fold by their seeding. Lawns may be advantageously dressed with stable manure in December, the long strawy portions being removed in March. On those portions of lawns, as around the house, where an immediate result in grass effect is desired, sod may be used. Fair sod can generally be had on roadsides, and if carefully taken up, and when laid down accurately jointed and solidified and covered with half an inch of rich compost, it will at once start off, and very soon be as much a fixture as the adjoining trees and shrubs. Lawn grass of good quality should produce a fair mat of herbage in from seventy to ninety days. Some persons offering lawn grass at a low price are using the so-called Canada Blue grass, which is not only worthless, but a pest, and difficult to eradicate.

Some people, after seeding a piece of land with lawn grass, expect to see a green mat in two or three weeks, but in this they are mistaken, as the better varieties of grass are slow to produce effect, and when an effect is quickly developed, it is at the expense of adaptability and permanency. For instance, a fine mat of green color can be had in two weeks from a heavy sowing of White Clover, something very effective and pleasing to the eye, but clover is not a grass, and is not suitable for lawns, failing to produce that velvet-like effect, the result of the growth of the erect leaves produced by the best grasses, which habit fits them to quickly recover after mowing. Manures or fertilizers for lawns may be of many combinations. We recommend, to those who prefer to do their own mixing, a compound of three hundred pounds of superphosphate, three hundred pounds dried meat, blood or fish, and four hundred pounds refuse common salt. The quantity of superphosphate and nitrogenous matter may be doubled, to advantage, or even made stronger, as grass will stand almost any amount of fertilizer. The common salt, used as an alterative and solvent, will be found to have a decided influence in keeping up the emerald green condition so desirable on a perfect lawn. Not more than three bushels to the acre should be applied in a season, and then best during a rain—never under a hot sun.

Old lawns, much in decay, are better if plowed up, leveled and resown, but often this course is not convenient, certainly not if the lawn can be renovated by a system taking less time. In that case, when prompt results are desirable, the old sod should be well combed by a harrow, to tear out the dried grass and easily extracted dead roots. This operation also breaks the earth, putting it in a pulverized condition to receive seed, which may be sown broadcast, which, falling between the living grass, roots into the friable and fresh soil, and is at once in position to germinate and occupy the space. On many lawns cut with the lawn mower there appear many pests—the Creeping Veronica and the Mouse-Eared Chickweed being prominent—which crowd out desirable grasses and mar the appearance of the sward. Under such circumstances it is advised to break up the parts affected and sow with seed of the Sheep Fescue, which will admit of such close cutting as to destroy all of the pestiferous plants.

INDEX.

Amateurs' garden	54, 55
Analyses of manures	41
April calendar	189
Asparagus	10
Asparagus beetle	58
August calendar	193
Bean fertilizer	32
Beans	2, 3, 10, 15, 165
Beets	52, 152
Bermuda grass	204
Berry baskets	15
Blackberry baskets	15, 43
Bloomsdale Swede	152
Blue grass	206, 209
Bone dust	31
Bordeaux mixture	68
Buffalo grass	203
Cabbage fungus	67
Cabbage insects	26, 62, 63
Cabbage, turnip-rooted	161
Calendar, monthly	185
Capital	5
Carrot	32, 52, 158, 161
Cauliflower	4
Celery	113
Census report	1
Central district	3
Chemical manures	30, 31, 35, 38
Chemistry of garden	30
Chili guano	39
Classification of weeds	83
Clover	212
Clover fertilizer	32
Club root	68
Cold frames	51, 84, 92
Commercial gardening	4
Compost	14, 35, 37
Costs	99, 132, 158
Covering seeds	42
Crates	15
Cross fertilization	75
Cucumber	2, 4, 10, 15, 32, 110, 165
Cultivation	20, 21, 155, 160
Cutworm	60
Damping off	100
December calendar	197
Desirable varieties	183
Destroying weeds	83
Dibble	53
Disclaimer, seedsmen's	79
Diseases of vegetables	65
Districts of vegetable culture	2
Drainage	19
Early crops	7
Egg plant	4, 52
Egg plants, treatment of	165
Emulsion, kerosene	64
Evaporation	20
Farmers	5
Farm expenses	5
February calendar	186
Fermenting lye	37
Fertile soils	19
Fertilizers	1, 3, 35, 37, 38, 40
Fish manure	40
Florida	3, 12
Forcing beds	71
Foreign weeds	82
Foxtail grass	206
Freight cars	168
Fumigation	110
Fungi	25, 130
Garden hoes	176
Gardening	1, 4, 22, 23, 27, 28, 29
Garden plan	55
Gardening under glass	94, 96, 99
Georgia	3
Germination	44, 48, 50, 80
Grafting	24
Grama grass	203
Grass	198, 203
Grass plants to the acre	210
Green fly	110
Greenhouse	25
Green manures	14, 33, 201
Growers of seed	76
Growth of vegetables	25
Guano	14, 38, 39
Half acre garden	181
Harvesting roots	148, 157
Heating	102
Heredity in plants	69, 72
Hessian fly	26
Hoes	176
Hotbeds	61, 84, 88
Implements	1, 14, 169
Insecticides	57
Insects	26, 57
Intermediate beds	51, 91
Irrigation	202
January calendar	185
July calendar	192
June calendar	191
Kale	2, 10
Kerosene emulsion	64
Kohl rabi	161
Labor	1, 101
Late crops	7
Lawn	213
Lettuce	45, 52, 103, 108

INDEX.

Lime 31
Location........................7, 17
Lupine 36
Lye, fermenting................. 37
Manures................35, 36, 87
Manures, green................. 33
Mangel wurzels..................154
March calendar 187
Market gardening..........2, 4, 94
May calendar......................190
Melons 10
Mixed grasses 207
Moisture 44
Monthly calendar...............185
Mulching............................... 53
Mushroom culture....135, 138, 139
New England district............. 2
Nitrate of soda..................... 31
Nitrogen 30, 31, 40
Nitrogenous plants............... 20
Norfolk district..................... 2
Novelties............................... 77
November calendar.............196
Oak 43
October calendar.................196
Oily seed 46
Onion fly............................... 64
Onions..................2, 45, 125, 132
Oranges 16
Orchard grass......................206
Over production................... 12
Packages..............................165
Packing vegetables..............164
Parsnip...........................52, 162
Pasture field........................208
Pea fungus........................... 68
Peas.................3, 10, 15, 16, 45, 68
Pepper.................................. 52
Perennial rye grass.............206
Perishable vegetables......7, 103
Peruvian guano................... 39
Philadelphia district............. 3
Phosphoric plants................ 30
Phosphate of lime................ 31
Plant pit............................... 93
Pollen.................................. 75
Potash....................30, 31, 32, 39
Potato bug........................... 60
Potato fertilizer................... 32
Potato plants....................... 30
Potato vine fungus............... 67
Potatoes.................2, 3, 10, 12, 16, 32
Products........................10, 110
Profit in gardening............1, 6
Profits...............................6, 9
Pulverization....................... 20
Quality................................168
Quantity of seed............42, 181
Quotations..........................108
Radishes......................2, 45, 52
Raspberries......................... 15
Red top grass 205, 208
Rental.................................. 7
Roots for stock feeding........140
Roots, saving......................147
Rotation 54
Rye 34, 201

Rye grass............................206
Salt....................................128
Saving roots.......................147
Saving seed......................... 74
Science of gardening............ 22
Seasons 3, 9, 11, 43
Seed beds............................ 51
Seed drills..............15, 128, 173
Seed testing........................ 46
Seeds 1, 41, 42, 46, 70, 73, 76, 134
Seeds in a pound.................209
Seedsmen's responsibilities...77, 79
September calendar............194
Sexes in plants.................... 69
Sheep farming....................200
Shipments..........................168
Shipping vegetables............164
Soil............8, 17, 18, 19, 103, 107, 112
Sorting vegetables..............166
South Atlanta district.......... 3
Sowing seeds..........41, 87, 90, 144
Spawn................................135
Spinach......................2, 10, 45
Squash................................ 10
Squash bug......................... 60
Stable manure.........13, 14, 35, 86
Starchy seed....................... 46
Storing...............................120
Strawberries.............10, 12, 15
Succession 54, 55
Sugar beets........................154
Sulphate of ammonia........... 31
Sun houses.........................111
Sunlight............................. 18
Superphosphate........13, 14, 31, 38
Systems 11
Tanks................................118
Testing seeds..................46, 47
Texas blue grass 204
Thinning out...................56, 146
Tillage......................17, 20, 21
Timothy......................204, 204
Tomatoes..........2, 3, 4, 10, 52, 168
Transplanting............51, 89, 111
Transportation.................7, 15
Trowel 56
Truck farming...................... 2
Turnip..................52, 142, 148, 150
Turnip fertilizer.................. 33
Turnip fly........................... 64
Value of products................ 2
Variability.......................... 71
Varieties of beet.................153
Varieties of carrot..............159
Varieties of onion...............126
Vegetables..............3, 4, 7, 65, 164
Ventilation..............102, 105, 165
Vitality..................45, 47, 50, 134
Watering............................100
Watermelon 3
Weeds...........................82, 83
Wheat fertilizer................... 32
White grub......................... 59
Winter vegetables 4
Wire worm.......................... 59
Wood ashes 31, 39
Wool 201

A Valuable Periodical for everybody in City, Village, and Country.

The American Agriculturist.

(ESTABLISHED 1842.)

THE LEADING INTERNATIONAL PUBLICATION
FOR THE
FARM, GARDEN, AND HOUSEHOLD.

A MONTHLY MAGAZINE of from 48 to 64 pages in each number, containing in each volume upward of 700 pages and over 1000 original engravings of typical and prize-winning Horses, Cattle, Sheep, Swine, and Fowls; New Fruits, Vegetables, and Flowers; House and Barn Plans; New Implements and Labor-saving Contrivances; and many pleasing and instructive pictures for young and old.

THE STANDARD AUTHORITY in all matters pertaining to Agriculture, Horticulture, and Rural Arts, and the oldest and most ably edited periodical of its class in the world.

BEST RURAL PERIODICAL IN THE WORLD.

The thousands of hints and suggestions given in every volume are prepared by practical, intelligent farmers, who know what they write about.

The Household Department is valuable to every housekeeper, affording very many useful hints and directions calculated to lighten and facilitate indoor work.

The Department for Children and Youth is prepared with special care, to furnish not only amusement, but also to inculcate knowledge and sound moral principles.

Subscription Terms: $1.50 a year, postage included; sample copies, 15c. each.

TRY IT A YEAR!

Address,

AMERICAN AGRICULTURIST,
52 & 54 Lafayette Place, New York.

SENT FREE ON APPLICATION.

DESCRIPTIVE CATALOGUE

—: OF :—

RURAL BOOKS,

Containing 116 8vo pages, profusely illustrated, and giving full descriptions of nearly 600 works on the following subjects:

FARM AND GARDEN,
　　　　FRUITS, FLOWERS, ETC.,
　　　　　　CATTLE, SHEEP, AND SWINE,
DOGS, ETC., HORSES, RIDING, ETC.,
　　　POULTRY, PIGEONS, AND BEES,
　　　　　　ANGLING AND FISHING,
BOATING, CANOEING, AND SAILING,
　　FIELD SPORTS AND NATURAL HISTORY,
　　　　　HUNTING, SHOOTING, ETC,
ARCHITECTURE AND BUILDING,
　　　LANDSCAPE GARDENING,
　　　　HOUSEHOLD AND MISCELLANEOUS.

PUBLISHERS AND IMPORTERS.

ORANGE JUDD COMPANY,

52 & 54 Lafayette Place, New York.

Mushrooms. How to Grow Them.

For home use fresh Mushrooms are a delicious, highly nutritious and wholesome delicacy; and for market they are less bulky than eggs, and, when properly handled, no crop is more remunerative. Anyone who has an ordinary house cellar, woodshed, or barn can grow Mushrooms. This is the most practical work on the subject ever written, and the only book on growing Mushrooms ever published in America. The whole subject is treated in detail, minutely and plainly, as only a practical man, actively engaged in Mushroom growing, can handle it. The author describes how he himself grows Mushrooms, and how they are grown for profit by the leading market gardeners, and for home use by the most successful private growers. The book is amply and pointedly illustrated, with engravings drawn from nature expressly for this work. By Wm. Falconer. Is nicely printed and bound in cloth. Price, post-paid.. 1.50

Allen's New American Farm Book.

The very best work on the subject; comprising all that can be condensed into an available volume. Originally by Richard L. Allen. Revised and greatly enlarged by Lewis F. Allen. Cloth, 12mo... 2.50

Henderson's Gardening for Profit.

By Peter Henderson. New edition. Entirely rewritten and greatly enlarged. The standard work on Market and Family Gardening. The successful experience of the author for more than thirty years, and his willingness to tell, as he does in this work, the secret of his success for the benefit of others, enables him to give most valuable information. The book is profusely illustrated. Cloth, 12mo... 2.00

Fuller's Practical Forestry.

A Treatise on the Propagation, Planting, and Cultivation, with a description and the botanical and proper names of all the indigenous trees of the United States, both Evergreen and Deciduous, with Notes on a large number of the most valuable Exotic Species. By Andrew S. Fuller, author of "Grape Culturist," "Small Fruit Culturist," etc. 1.50

The Dairyman's Manual.

By Henry Stewart, author of "The Shepherd's Manual," "Irrigation," etc. A useful and practical work by a writer who is well known as thoroughly familiar with the subject of which he writes. Cloth, 12mo.. 2.00

Truck Farming at the South.

A work giving the experience of a successful grower of vegetables or "grain truck" for Northern markets. Essential to any one who contemplates entering this promising field of Agriculture. By A. Oemler, of Georgia. Illustrated. Cloth, 12mo............................ 1.50

Harris on the Pig.

New edition. Revised and enlarged by the author. The points of the various English and American breeds are thoroughly discussed, and the great advantage of using thoroughbred males clearly shown. The work is equally valuable to the farmer who keeps but few pigs, and to the breeder on an extensive scale. By Joseph Harris. Illustrated. Cloth, 12mo 1.50

Jones's Peanut Plant—Its Cultivation and Uses.

A practical Book, instructing the beginner how to raise good crops of Peanuts. By B. W. Jones, Surry Co., Va. Paper Cover,..... .50

Barry's Fruit Garden.
By P. Barry. A standard work on fruit and fruit-trees; the author having had over thirty years' practical experience at the head of one of the largest nurseries in this country. New edition, revised up to date. Invaluable to all fruit-growers. Illustrated. Cloth, 12mo. 2.00

The Propagation of Plants.
By Andrew S. Fuller. Illustrated with numerous engravings. An eminently practical and useful work. Describing the process of hybridizing and crossing species and varieties, and also the many different modes by which cultivated plants may be propagated and multiplied. Cloth, 12mo... 1.50

Stewart's Shepherd's Manual.
A Valuable Practical Treatise on the Sheep, for American farmers and sheep growers. It is so plain that a farmer, or a farmer's son, who has never kept a sheep may learn from its pages how to manage a flock successfully, and yet so complete that even the experienced shepherd may gather many suggestions from it. The results of personal experience of some years with the characters of the various modern breeds of sheep, and the sheep-raising capabilities of many portions of our extensive territory and that of Canada—and the careful study of the diseases to which our sheep are chiefly subject, with those by which they may eventually be afflicted through unforeseen accidents—as well as the methods of management called for under our circumstances, are here gathered. By Henry Stewart. Illustrated. Cloth, 12mo. ... 1.50

Allen's American Cattle.
Their History, Breeding, and Management. By Lewis F. Allen. This Book will be considered indispensable by every breeder of live stock. The large experience of the author in improving the character of American herds adds to the weight of his observations, and has enabled him to produce a work which will at once make good his claims as a standard authority on the subject. New and revised edition. Illustrated. Cloth, 12mo.............................. 2.50

Fuller's Grape Culturist.
By A. S. Fuller. This is one of the very best of works on the culture of the hardy grapes, with full directions for all departments of propagation, culture, etc., with 150 excellent engravings, illustrating planting, training, grafting, etc. Cloth, 12mo.......................... 1.50

White's Cranberry Culture.
CONTENTS:—Natural History.—History of Cultivation.—Choice of Location.—Preparing the Ground.—Planting the Vines.—Management of Meadows.—Flooding—Enemies and Difficulties Overcome.—Picking.—Keeping.—Profit and Loss.—Letters from Practical Growers.—Insects Injurious to the Cranberry. By Joseph J. White. A practical grower. Illustrated. Cloth, 12mo. New and revised edition. 1.25

Herbert's Hints to Horse-Keepers.
This is one of the best and most popular works on the Horse in this country. A Complete Manual for Horsemen, embracing: How to Breed a Horse; How to Buy a Horse; How to Break a Horse; How to Use a Horse; How to Feed a Horse; How to Physic a Horse (Allopathy or Homœopathy); How to Groom a Horse; How to Drive a Horse; How to Ride a Horse, etc. By the late Henry William Herbert (Frank Forester). Beautifully Illustrated. Cloth, 12mo... 1.75

Henderson's Practical Floriculture.

By Peter Henderson. A guide to the successful propagation and cultivation of florists' plants. The work is not one for florists and gardeners only, but the amateur's wants are constantly kept in mind, and we have a very complete treatise on the cultivation of flowers under glass, or in the open air, suited to those who grow flowers for pleasure as well as those who make them a matter of trade. The work is characterized by the same radical common sense that marked the author's "Gardening for Profit," and it holds a high place in the estimation of lovers of agriculture. Beautifully illustrated. New and enlarged edition. Cloth, 12mo 1.50

Harris's Talks on Manures.

By Joseph Harris, M. S., author of "Walks and Talks on the Farm," "Harris on the Pig." etc. Revised and enlarged by the author. A series of familiar and practical talks between the author and the deacon, the doctor, and other neighbors, on the whole subject of manures and fertilizers; including a chapter specially written for it by Sir John Bennet Lawes, of Rothamsted, England. Cloth, 12mo 1.75

Waring's Draining for Profit and Draining for Health.

This book is a very complete and practical treatise, the directions in which are plain, and easily followed. The subject of thorough farm drainage is discussed in all its bearings, and also that more extensive land drainage by which the sanitary condition of any district may be greatly improved, even to the banishment of fever and ague, typhoid and malarious fever. By Geo. E. Waring, Jr Illustrated, Cloth 12mo.
1.50

The Practical Rabbit-Keeper.

By Cuniculus. Illustrated. A comprehensive work on keeping and raising Rabbits for pleasure as well as for profit. The book is abundantly illustrated with all the various Courts, Warrens, Hutches, Fencing, etc., and also with excellent portraits of the most important species of rabbits throughout the world. 12mo 1.50

Quinby's New Bee-Keeping.

The Mysteries of Bee-keeping Explained. Combining the results of Fifty Years' Experience, with the latest discoveries and inventions, and presenting the most approved methods, forming a complete work. Cloth, 12mo 1.50

Profits in Poultry.

Useful and Ornamental Breeds and their Profitable Management. This excellent work contains the combined experience of a number of practical men in all departments of poultry raising. It is profusely illustrated and forms an unique and important addition to our poultry literature. Cloth, 12mo 1.00

Barn Plans and Outbuildings.

Two Hundred and Fifty-seven Illustrations. A most Valuable Work, full of Ideas, Hints, Suggestions, Plans, etc., for the Construction of Barns and Outbuildings, by Practical writers. Chapters are devoted, among other subjects, to the Economic Erection and Use of Barns. Grain Barns, House Barns, Cattle Barns, Sheep Barns, Corn Houses, Smoke Houses, Ice Houses, Pig Pens, Granaries, etc. There are likewise chapters upon Bird Houses, Dog Houses, Tool Sheds, Ventilators, Roofs and Roofing, Doors and Fastenings, Work Shops, Poultry Houses, Manure Sheds, Barn Yards, Root Pits, etc. Recently published. Cloth, 12mo 1.50

STANDARD BOOKS. 5

Parsons on the Rose.
By Samuel B. Parsons. A treatise on the propagation, culture, and history of the rose. New and revised edition. In his work upon the rose, Mr. Parsons has gathered up the curious legends concerning the flower, and gives us an idea of the esteem in which it was held in former times. A simple garden classification has been adopted, and the leading varieties under each class enumerated and briefly described. The chapters on multiplication, cultivation, and training are very full, and the work is altogether one of the most complete before the public. Illustrated. Cloth, 12mo......................1.00

Heinrich's Window Flower Garden.
The author is a practical florist, and this enterprising volume embodies his personal experiences in Window Gardening during a long period. New and enlarged edition. By Julius J. Heinrich. Fully Illustrated. Cloth, 12mo..75

Liautard's Chart of the Age of the Domestic Animals.
Adopted by the United States Army. Enables one to accurately determine the age of horses, cattle, sheep, dogs, and pigs............50

Pedder's Land Measurer for Farmers.
A convenient Pocket Companion, showing at once the contents of any piece of land, when its length and width are known, up to 1,500 feet either way, with various other useful farm tables. Cloth, 18mo; .60

How to Plant and What to Do with the Crops.
With other valuable hints for the Farm, Garden and Orchard. By Mark W. Johnson. Illustrated. CONTENTS: Times for Sowing Seeds; Covering Seeds; Field Crops; Garden or Vegetable Seeds, Sweet Herbs, etc.; Tree Seeds; Flower Seeds; Fruit Trees; Distances Apart for Fruit Trees and Shrubs; Profitable Farming; Green or Manuring Crops; Root Crops; Forage Plants; What to do with the Crops; The Rotation of Crops; Varieties; Paper Covers, post-paid...........50

Your Plants.
Plain and Practical Directions for the Treatment of Tender and Hardy Plants in the House and in the Garden. By James Sheehan. The above title well describes the character of the work—"Plain and Practical." The author, a commercial florist and gardener, has endeavored, in this work, to answer the many questions asked by his customers, as to the proper treatment of plants. The book shows all through that its author is a practical man, and he writes as one with a large store of experience. The work better meets the wants of the amateur who grows a few plants in the window, or has a small flower Garden, than a larger treatise intended for those who cultivate plants upon a more extended scale. Price, post-paid, paper covers..................40

Husmann's American Grape-Growing and Wine-Making.
By George Husmann of Talcoa vineyards, Napa, California. New and enlarged edition. With contributions from well-known grape-growers, giving a wide range of experience. The author of this book is a recognized authority on the subject. Cloth, 12mo.............. 1.50

The Scientific Angler.
A general and instructive work on Artistic Angling, by the late David Foster. Compiled by his Sons. With an Introductory Chapter and Copious Foot Notes, by William C. Harris, Editor of the "American Angler." Cloth, 12mo.. 1.50

Keeping One Cow.
A collection of Prize Essays, and selections from a number of other Essays, with editorial notes, suggestions, etc. This book gives the latest information, and in a clear and condensed form, upon the management of a single Milch Cow. Illustrated with full-page engravings of the most famous dairy cows. Recently published. Cloth, 12mo 1.00

Law's Veterinary Adviser
A Guide to the Prevention and Treatment of Disease in Domestic Animals. This is one of the best works on this subject, and is especially designed to supply the need of the busy American Farmer, who can rarely avail himself of the advice of a Scientific Veterinarian. It is brought up to date and treats of the Prevention of Disease, as well as of the Remedies. By Prof. Jas. Law. Cloth, Crown 8vo 3.00

Guenon's Treatise on Milch Cows.
A Treatise on the Bovine Species in General. An entirely new translation of the last edition of this popular and instructive book. By Thos. J. Hand, Secretary of the American Jersey Cattle Club. With over 100 Illustrations, especially engraved for this work. Cloth, 12mo. 1.00

The Cider Maker's Handbook.
A complete guide for making and keeping pure cider. By J. M. Trowbridge. Fully Illustrated. Cloth, 12mo 1.00

Long's Ornamental Gardening for Americans.
A treatise on Beautifying Homes, Rural Districts, and Cemeteries. A plain and practical work at a moderate price, with numerous illustrations, and instructions so plain that they may be readily followed. By Elias A. Long. Landscape Architect. Illustrated. Cloth, 12mo. 2.00

The Dogs of Great Britain, America and Other Countries.
New, enlarged and revised edition. Their breeding, training and management, in health and disease; comprising all the essential parts of the two standard works on the dog, by "Stonehenge," thereby furnishing for $2 what once cost $11.25. Contains Lists of all Premiums given at the last Dog Shows. It Describes the Best Game and Hunting Grounds in America. Contains over One Hundred Beautiful Engravings, embracing most noted Dogs in both Continents, making together, with Chapters by American Writers, the most Complete Dog Book ever published. Cloth, 12mo 2.00

Stewart's Feeding Animals.
By Elliot W. Stewart. A new and valuable practical work upon the laws of animal growth, specially applied to the rearing and feeding horses, cattle, diary cows, sheep and swine. Illustrated. Cloth, 12mo. 2.00

How to Co-operate.
A Manual for Co-operators. By Herbert Myrick. This book describes the how rather than the wherefore of co-operation. In other words it tells how to manage a co-operative store, farm or factory, and co-operative dairying, banking and fire insurance, and co-operative farmers' and women's exchanges for both buying and selling. The directions given are based on the actual experience of successful co-operative enterprises in all parts of the United States. The character and usefulness of the book commend it to the attention of all men and women who desire to better their condition. 12mo. Cloth 1.50

Batty's Practical Taxidermy and Home Decoration.
By Joseph H. Batty, taxidermist for the government surveys and many colleges and museums in the United States. An entirely new and complete as well as authentic work on taxidermy—giving in detail full directions for collecting and mounting animals, birds, reptiles, fish, insects, and general objects of natural history. 125 illustrations. Cloth, 12mo.. 1.50

Stewart's Irrigation for the Farm, Garden, and Orchard.
New and Enlarged Edition. This work is offered to those American Farmers, and other cultivators of the soil, who from painful experience can readily appreciate the losses which result from the scarcity of water at critical periods. By Henry Stewart. Fully illustrated. Cloth, 12mo.. 1.50

Johnson's How Crops Grow.
New Edition, entirely rewritten. A Treatise on the Chemical Composition, Structure, and Life of the Plant. Revised Edition. This book is a guide to the knowledge of agricultural plants, their composition, their structure, and modes of development and growth; of the complex organization of plants, and the use of the parts; the germination of seeds, and the food of plants obtained both from the air and the soil. The book is an invaluable one to all real students of agriculture. With numerous illustrations and tables of analysis. By Prof. Samuel W. Johnson, of Yale College. Cloth, 12mo............. 2.00

Johnson's How Crops Feed.
A treatise on the Atmosphere and the Soil, as related in the Nutrition of Agricultural Plants. The volume—the companion and complement to "How Crops Grow,"—has been welcomed by those who appreciate scientific aspects of agriculture. Illustrated. By Prof. Samuel W. Johnson. Cloth, 12mo.. 2.00

Warington's Chemistry of the Farm.
Treating with the utmost clearness and conciseness, and in the most popular manner possible, of the relations of Chemistry to Agriculture, and providing a welcome manual for those, who, while not having time to systematically study Chemistry, will gladly have such an idea as this gives them of its relation to operations on the farm. By R. Warington, F. C. S. Cloth, 12mo................................ 1.00

French's Farm Drainage.
The Principles, Process, and Effects of Draining Land, with Stones, Wood, Ditch-plows, Open Ditches, and especially with Ties; including Tables of Rainfall, Evaporation, Filtration, Excavation, Capacity of Pipes, cost and number to the acre. By Judge French, of New Hampshire. Cloth, 12mo................................... 1.50

Hunter and Trapper.
The best modes of Hunting and Trapping are fully explained, and Foxes, Deer, Bears, etc., fall into his traps readily by following his directions. By Halsey Thrasher, an old and experienced sportsman. Cloth, 12mo... .75

The American Merino. For Wool or for Mutton.
A practical and most valuable work on the selection, care, breeding and diseases of the Merino sheep, in all sections of the the United States. It is a full and exhaustive treatise upon this one breed of sheep. By Stephen Powers. Cloth, 12mo..................... 1.

Armatage's Every Man His Own Horse Doctor.
By Prof. George Armatage, M. R. C. V. S. A valuable and comprehensive guide for both the professional and general reader with the fullest and latest information regarding all diseases, local injuries, lameness, operations, poisons, the dispensatory, etc., etc., with practical anatomical and surgical Illustrations. New Edition. Together with Blaine's "Veterinary Art," and numerous recipes. One large 8vo. volume, 830 pages, half morocco............................ 7.50

Dadd's Modern Horse Doctor.
Containing Practical Observations on the Causes, Nature, and Treatment of Diseases and Lameness of Horses—embracing recent and improved Methods, according to an enlightened system of Veterinary Practice, for Preservation and Restoration of Health. Illustrated. By Geo. H. Dadd, M. D. V. S., Cloth, 12mo.................... 1.50

The Family Horse.
Its Stabling, Care, and Feeding. By Geo. A. Martin. A Practical Manual, full of the most useful information. Illustrated. Cloth, 12mo 1.00

Sander's Horse Breeding.
Being the general principles of Heredity applied to the Business of Breeding Horses and the Management of Stallions, Brood Mares and Foals. The book embraces all that the breeder should know in regard to the selection of stock, management of the stallion, brood mare, and foal, and treatment of diseases peculiar to breeding animals. By J. H. Sanders. 12mo, cloth.. 2.00

Coburn's Swine Husbandry.
New, revised and enlarged edition. The Breeding, Rearing and Management of Swine, and the Prevention and Treatment of their Diseases. It is the fullest and freshest compendium relating to Swine Breeding yet offered. By F. D. Coburn. Cloth, 12mo......... 1.75

Dadd's American Cattle Doctor.
By George H. Dadd, M. D., Veterinary Practitioner. To help every man to be his own cattle-doctor; giving the necessary information for preserving the health and curing the diseases of oxen, cows, sheep, and swine, with a great variety of original recipes, and valuable information on farm and dairy management. Cloth, 12mo............ 1.50

Silos, Ensilage, and Silage.
A practical treatise on the Ensilage of Fodder Corn. Containing the most recent and authentic information on this important subject, by Manly Miles, M.D., F.R.M.S. Illustrated. Cloth 12mo......... .50

Broom Corn and Brooms.
A Treatise on Raising Broom-Corn and Making Brooms on a small or Large Scale. Illustrated. 12mo. Cloth cover................... .50

American Bird Fancier.
Or how to breed, rear, and care for Song and Domestic Birds. This valuable and important little work for all who are interested in the keeping of Song Birds, has been revised and enlarged, and is now a complete manual upon the subject. All who own valuable birds, or wish to do so, will find the new Fancier indispensable. New, revised and enlarged edition. By D. J. Browne, and Dr. Fuller Walker. Illustrated, paper cover... .50

Armatage's Every Man His Own Cattle Doctor.
The Veterinary Cyclopedia—Embracing all the practical information of value heretofore published on the Diseases of Cattle, Sheep, and Swine, together with the latest and best information regarding all known diseases up to the present time. Compiled and edited by that eminent authority, Prof. George Armatage, M. R. C. V. S. One large octavo volume, 894 pages, with upwards of 350 practical illustrations, showing forms of disease and treatment. Half morocco. 7.50

Onions—How to Raise them Profitably.
Being the Practical Details, from Selection of Seed and Preparation of Ground to Harvesting and Marketing the Crop, given very plainly by Seventeen Practical Onion Growers of long experience residing in different parts of the country. No more valuable work of its size was ever issued. Paper cover, 8vo............................ .20

Tobacco Culture—Full Practical Details.
This useful and valuable work contains full details of every process from the Selection and Preparation of the Seed and Soil to the Harvesting, Curing and Marketing the Crop, with illustrative engravings of the operations. The work was prepared by Fourteen Experienced Tobacco Growers, residing in different parts of the country. It also contains notes on the Tobacco Worm, with illustrations, 8vo,.. .25

Hop Culture.
Plain directions given by ten experienced cultivators. Revised, enlarged and edited by A. S. Fuller. Forty engravings............ .30

Flax Culture.
A very valuable work, containing full directions, from selection of ground and seed to preparation and marketing of crop, as given by a number of experienced growers, 8vo........................ .30

Potato Pests.
No Farmer can afford to be without this little book. It gives the most complete account of the Colorado Beetle anywhere to be found, and includes all the latest discoveries as to the habits of the insect and the various means for its destruction. It is well illustrated, and exhibits in a map the spread of the insect since it left its native home. By Prof. C. V. Riley. Paper cover.............................. .50

Home Fishing and Home Waters.
By Seth Green. The Utilization of Farm Streams; Management of Fish in the Artificial Pond; Transportation of Eggs and Fry, etc. Cloth, 12mo... .50

Reed's House Plans for Everybody.
By S. B. Reed. This useful volume meets the wants of persons of moderate means, and gives a wide range of design, from a dwelling costing $250 up to $8,000, and adapted to farm, village and town residences. Nearly all of these plans have been tested by practical workings. One feature of the work imparts a value over any similar publication of the kind that we have seen. It gives an estimate of the quantity of every article used in the construction, and the cost of each article at the time the building was erected or the design made. Even if prices vary from time to time, one can, from these data, ascertain within a few dollars the probable cost of constructing any one of the buildings here presented. Profusely illustrated. Cloth, black and gold, 12mo... 1.50

Gregory on Cabbages—How to Grow Them.
A Practical Treatise on Cabbage Culture, giving full details on every point, including Keeping and Marketing the Crop. By James J. H. Gregory. Paper cover, 12mo... .30

Gregory on Carrots, Mangold-Wurtzels, etc.
How to raise them, how to keep them, and how to feed them. By J. J. H. Gregory. Paper Cover, 12mo................................ .30

Gregory on Onion Raising.
What kinds to raise, and the way to raise them. By J. J. H. Gregory. Paper cover, 12mo... .30

Gregory on Squashes.
This Treatise, which no Farmer or Gardener ought to be without, tells all about selecting the soil for squashes; how much Manure is necessary; how to prepare and Plant; about Hoeing and Cultivating; Setting of the Fruit; Ripening, Gathering, Storing, Care during Winter, etc. By J. J. H. Gregory. Paper cover, 12mo................. .30

Hog-Raising and Pork-Making.
By Rufus Bacon Martin. The hog is reared for the money that is in him, and he represents either a profit or loss to his owner according to the treatment he receives. This pamphlet gives the personal research and experience of the author, contains many valuable suggestions, and answers many of the questions that arise in the business of hog-raising. Paper, 12mo... .40

Fulton's Peach Culture.
This is the only practical guide to Peach Culture on the Delaware Peninsula, and is the best work upon the subject of peach growing for those who would be successful in that culture in any part of the country. It has been thoroughly revised and a large portion of it rewritten, by Hon. J. Alexander Fulton, the author, bringing it down to date. Cloth, 12mo.. 1.50

Silk Culture.
A Handbook for Silk-Growers. By Mrs. C. E. Bamford. Contents.—Chapter I. The Mulberry.—II. Gathering the Leaves.—III. The Cocoonery.—IV. Eggs of the Silk Worm Moth.—V. Feeding the Silk Worms.—VI. Moulting.—VII. Spinning.—VIII. The Cocoons.—IX. The Moths of the Silk Worm.—X. Varieties of Silk Worms.—XI. Diseases of the Silk Worm.—XII. Reeling.—XIII. Chemistry of Silk.—XIV. Miscellaneous. Paper, 12mo. Price, postpaid... .30

Treats' Injurious Insects of the Farm and Garden. By Mrs. Mary Treat.
An original investigator who has added much to our knowledge of both Plants and insects, and those who are familiar with Darwin's works are aware that he gives her credit for important observation and discoveries. New and Enlarged Edition. With an Illustrated Chapter on Beneficial Insects. Fully illustrated. Cloth, 12mo............ 2.00

Fuller's Small Fruit Culturist.
By Andrew S. Fuller. Rewritten, enlarged, and brought fully up to the present time. The book covers the whole ground of propagating small fruits, their culture, varieties, packing for market, etc. It is very finely and thoroughly illustrated, and makes an admirable companion to "The Grape Culturist," by the same well known author.
1.50

www.ingramcontent.com/pod-product-compliance
Lightning Source LLC
Chambersburg PA
CBHW022012220426
43663CB00007B/1049